The Oxford Christmas Book For Children

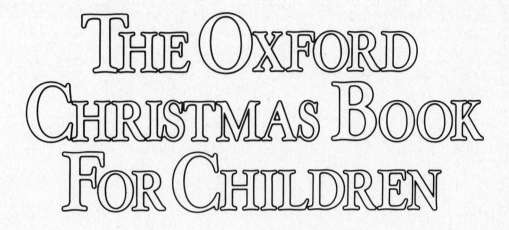

Roderick Hunt

Oxford University Press

To Sarah, Rebecca, John, Philip and David

Oxford University Press, Walton Street, Oxford OX2 6DP
London   Glasgow   New York   Toronto
Delhi   Bombay   Calcutta   Madras   Karachi
Kuala Lumpur   Singapore   Hong Kong   Tokyo
Nairobi   Dar es Salaam   Cape Town   Salisbury
Melbourne   Wellington
and associate companies in
Beirut   Berlin   Ibadan   Mexico City

British Library Cataloguing in Publication Data
The Oxford Christmas book for children.
1. Christmas – Juvenile literature
I. Hunt, Roderick
394.2'68282   GT4985

ISBN 0–19–278104–9

Phototypeset by Tradespools Limited, Frome, Somerset
Printed in Great Britain by
William Clowes (Beccles) Limited
Beccles and London

And it came to pass in those days, that there went out a decree from Caesar Augustus, that all the world should be taxed. (And this taxing was first made when Cyrenius was governor of Syria.) And all went to be taxed, every one into his own city. And Joseph also went up from Galilee, out of the city of Nazareth, into Judaea, unto the city of David, which is called Bethlehem; (because he was of the house and lineage of David:) to be taxed with Mary his espoused wife, being great with child. And so it was, that, while they were there, the days were accomplished that she should be delivered. And she brought forth her firstborn son, and wrapped him in swaddling clothes, and laid him in a manger; because there was no room for them in the inn.

And there were in the same country shepherds abiding in the field, keeping watch over their flock by night. And, lo, the angel of the Lord came upon them, and the glory of the Lord shone round about them: and they were sore afraid. And the angel said unto them, Fear not: for, behold, I bring you good tidings of great joy, which shall be to all people. For unto you is born this day in the city of David a Saviour, which is Christ the Lord. And this shall be a sign unto you; Ye shall find the babe wrapped in swaddling clothes, lying in a manger. And suddenly there was with the angel a multitude of the heavenly host praising God, and saying, Glory to God in the highest, and on earth peace, good will toward men.

And it came to pass, as the angels were gone away from them into heaven, the shepherds said one to another, Let us now go even unto Bethlehem, and see this thing which is come to pass, which the Lord hath made known unto us. And they came with haste, and found Mary, and Joseph, and the babe lying in a manger. And when they had seen it, they made known abroad the saying which was told them concerning this child. And all they that heard it wondered at those things which were told them by the shepherds. But Mary kept all these things, and pondered them in her heart. And the shepherds returned, glorifying and praising God for all the things that they had heard and seen, as it was told unto them.

St Luke 2: 1–20

Contents

Which of the Nine?

Once upon a time in the city of Budapest there lived a poor shoemaker who simply couldn't make ends meet. Not because the people had suddenly decided to give up wearing shoes, nor because the city council had passed an ordinance directing that his shoes be sold at half price, nor even because his work was not satisfactory. Indeed, the good man did such excellent work that his customers actually complained that they couldn't wear out anything he had once sewed together. He had plenty of customers who paid him promptly and well enough; not one of them had run away without paying his bill. And yet Cobbler John couldn't make ends meet.

The reason was that the good Lord had blessed him all too plentifully with nine children, all of them healthy as acorns.

Then one day, as if Cobbler John hadn't trouble enough, his wife died. Cobbler John was left alone in this world with nine children. Two or three of them were going to school; one or two of them were being tutored; one had to be carried around; gruel had to be cooked for the next; another one had to be fed; the next one dressed, yet another washed. And on top of all this he had to earn a living for them all. As you can imagine this was a big job—just in case you doubt it.

When shoes were made for them, nine had to be made all at once; when bread was sliced, nine slices had to be cut all at one time. When beds were made ready, the entire room between the window and door became one single bed, full of little and big blonde and brunette heads.

'Oh my dear Lord God, how Thou hast blessed me,' the good artisan often sighed. And even after midnight he still worked and hammered away at his lasts in order to feed the bodies of so many souls, stopping occasionally to chide now one, now another tossing restlessly in a dream. Nine they were—a round number, nine. But thanks to the Lord, there was no cause for complaint because all nine were healthy, obedient, beautiful and well-behaved, blessed with sound bodies and stomachs.

On Christmas Eve, Cobbler John returned late from his many errands. He had delivered all sorts of finished work and had collected a little money which he had used to buy supplies and pay for their daily needs. Hurrying homeward he saw stands on every street corner, laden with golden and silver lambs and candy dolls which push-cart women were selling as gifts for well-behaved children. Cobbler John stopped before one or two of the carts . . . Maybe he ought to buy something . . . but what? For all nine? That would cost too much. Then just for one? And make the others envious? No, he'd give them another kind of present: a beautiful and good one, one that would neither break nor wear out, and which all could enjoy together and not take away from each other.

'Well, children! One, two, three, four . . . are you all here?' he said when he arrived home within the circle of his family of nine. 'Do you know it is Christmas Eve? A holiday, a very special holiday. Tonight we do no work, we just rejoice!'

'The children were so happy to hear that they were supposed to rejoice that they almost tore down the house.

'What now! Let's see if I can't teach you that beautiful song I know. It's a very beautiful song. I have saved it to give you all a Christmas present.'

The little ones crawled noisily into their father's lap and up on his shoulders, and waited eagerly to hear the lovely song.

'Now what did I tell you? If you are *good* children . . . just stand nicely in line . . . there . . . the bigger ones over here and the smaller ones next to them.' He stood them in a row like organ pipes, letting the two youngest ones stay on his lap.

'And now—silence! First I'll sing it through, then you can join in.' Taking off his green cap and assuming a serious, pious expression, Cobbler John began to sing the beautiful melody: 'On the blessed birth of Our Lord Jesus Christ . . .'

The bigger boys and girls learned it very quickly, but the smaller ones found it a bit more difficult. They were always off key and out of rhythm. But after a while they all knew it. And there could be no more joyous sound than when all the nine thin little voices sang together that glorious song of the angels on that memorable night. Perhaps the angels were still singing it when the melodious voices of the nine innocent souls prayed for an echo from above. For surely there is gladness in heaven over the song of children.

But there was less gladness immediately above them. There was a bachelor living all by himself in nine rooms. In one he sat, in another he slept, in the third one he smoked his pipe, in the fourth he dined, and who knows what he did in the others? This man had neither wife nor children but more money than he could count. Sitting in room number eight that night, the rich man was wondering why life had lost its taste. Why did his soft, springy bed give him no peaceful dreams? Then, from Cobbler John's room below, at first faintly but with ever increasing strength, came the strains of a certain joy-inspiring song. At first he tried not to listen, thinking they would soon stop. But when they started all over for the tenth time, he could stand it no longer. Crushing out his expensive cigar, he went down in his dressing-gown to the shoemaker's flat.

They had just come to the end of a verse when he walked in. Cobbler John respectfully got up from his three-legged stool and greeted the great gentleman.

'You are John, the cobbler, aren't you?' the rich man asked.

'That I am, and at your service, Your Excellency. Do you wish to order a pair of patent-leather boots?'

'That isn't why I came. How very many children you have!'

'Indeed I have, Your Excellency—little ones and great big ones. Quite a few mouths to feed!'

'And many more mouths when they sing! Look here, Master John, I'd like to do you a favour. Give me one of your children. I'll adopt him, educate him as my own son, take him travelling abroad with me, and make him into a gentleman. One day he'll be able to help the rest of you.'

Cobbler John stared when he heard this. These were big words—to have one of his children made a gentleman! Who wouldn't be taken by such an idea? Why, of course he'd let him have one! What good fortune! How could he refuse?

'Well then, pick out one of them quickly, and let's get it over with,' said the gentleman. Cobbler John started to choose.

'This one here is Alex. No, him I couldn't let go. He is a good student and I want him to become a priest. The next one? That's a girl and, of course, Your Excellency doesn't want a girl. Little Ferenc? He already helps me with my work. I couldn't do without him. Johnny? There, there—he is named after me. I couldn't very well give him away! Joseph? He's the image of his mother—it's as if I saw her every time I look at him. This place wouldn't be the same without him. And the next one is another girl—she wouldn't do. Then comes little Paul: he was his mother's favourite. Oh my poor darling would turn in her grave if I gave him away. And the last two are small—they'd be too much trouble for Your Excellency . . .'

He had reached the end of the line without being able to choose. Now he started all over; this time beginning with the youngest and ending with the oldest. But the result was always the same: he couldn't decide which one to give away because one was as dear to him as the other, and he would miss them all.

'Come, my little ones—you do the choosing,' he finally said. 'Which of you wants to go away and become a gentleman and travel in style? Come now, speak up! Who wants to go?'

The poor shoemaker was on the verge of tears as he asked them. But while he was encouraging them, the children slowly slipped behind their father's back, each taking hold of him; his hand, his arm, his leg, his coat, his apron, all hanging on to him and hiding from the gentleman. Finally, Cobbler John couldn't control himself any longer. He knelt down, gathered all into his arms and let his tears fall on their heads as they cried with him.

'It can't be done, Your Excellency! It can't be done. Ask of me anything in the world, but I can't give you a single one of my children so long as the Good Lord has given them to me.'

The rich gentleman said that he understood, but that the shoemaker should do at least one thing for him: would he and his children please not sing any more? And for this single sacrifice he asked Cobbler John to accept one thousand florins.

Master John had never heard the words 'One thousand florins' spoken in all his life. Now he felt the money being pressed into his hand.

His Excellency went back to his room and to his boredom. And Cobbler John stood staring incredulously at the oddly-shaped bank note. Then he fearfully locked it away in the wooden chest, put the key in his pocket, and was silent. The little ones were silent too. Singing was forbidden. The older children slumped moodily in their chairs, quieting the smaller ones by telling them they weren't allowed to sing any more because it disturbed the fine gentleman upstairs. Cobbler John himself was silently walking up and down. Impatiently he pushed aside little Paul, the one who had been his wife's favourite, when the boy asked that he be taught that beautiful song because he had already forgotten how it went.

'We aren't allowed to sing any more!'

Then he sat down angrily at his bench and bent intently over his work. He cut and hammered and sewed until suddenly he caught himself singing: 'On the blessed birth of Our Lord Jesus Christ . . .' He clapped his hand over his mouth. But then, all at once he was very angry. He banged the hammer down on the work-bench, kicked his stool from under him, opened the chest, took out the thousand florin note and ran upstairs to His Excellency's apartment.

'Good kind Excellency, I am your most humble servant. Please take back your money! Let it not be mine, but let us sing whenever we please, because to stop me and my children is worth much more than a thousand florins.'

With that, he put the note down on the table and rushed breathlessly back to his waiting children. He kissed them, one after the other, and, lining them up in a row, just like organ pipes, he sat himself on a low stool, and together they began to sing again with heart and soul: 'On the blessed birth of Our Lord Jesus Christ . . .'

They couldn't have been happier if they had owned the whole of the great big house.

But the one who owned the house was pacing up and down through his nine rooms, asking himself how it was that people down below could be so happy and full of joy in such a tiresome boring world as this!

Make your own Crèche

The basic form for each figure is made from a rectangle of silver foil. Tear it as shown here.

Use your fingers to crush the foil into a human or animal shape. 15 to 20 centimetres is a good height for the human figures.

The animals can then be made in proportion.

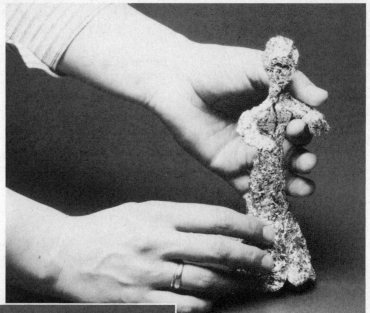

Build up each figure with kitchen paper strips soaked in wallpaper paste wrapped round your foil. Cover it well and overlap for strength. Three layers should be enough.

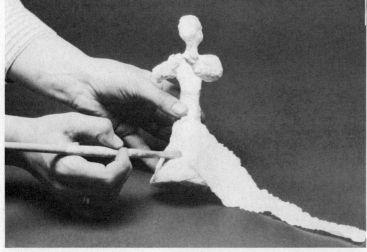

Put on features with bits of the paper towel soaked in paste.

Costumes can be made out of kitchen towelling soaked in the same paste and draped on the figure to give a feeling of Biblical costumes.

Paint your figures and glue on lace and small jewels to add texture and a regal note.

13

An Advent Decoration

On the four Sundays leading up to Christmas (called Advent Sundays) people begin to think about the Advent, or 'coming' of the Lord. In churches, and in many homes, Advent is marked by the lighting of candles, one for each Sunday before Christmas. In Germany, an Advent wreath of evergreens and one red candle is hung up on the first Advent Sunday. Each Sunday a candle is added, and every day a paper star, bearing a Bible passage, is hung on the wreath. Advent houses or calendars are very popular. They remind children of the days until Christmas. The Advent calendar is a picture made of thin card with twenty-five windows. The windows are numbered, so that one can be opened on each day of the Advent weeks.

Make this unusual Advent calendar and wall decoration to mark the days until Christmas.

(For a colour photograph of the Advent calendar, see pp. 34–5.)

You will need:
a large polystyrene ball (you can buy these at florists or garden centres), OR a thick piece of polystyrene (the sort used for packing)
twenty-five brightly coloured pencils OR the same number of thin garden canes (the green type)
old used Christmas cards,
thin white card,
felt tip pens, latex glue,
coloured paper or felt.

To make the calendar:
Cut the polystyrene ball in half, OR cut a circular disc from the thick polystyrene. (You may find a serrated edged knife will be best to do this.) Cut the disc about 12cm in diameter.
Trace the five-pointed star from the templates on page 158 and trace it on to the felt or coloured paper. Stick the star on to your shape with latex glue.

Take the pencils and push the sharp ends evenly into the foam shape. (If you are using garden canes, you may need to shorten them and sharpen the ends.)

Cut out twenty-five circle pictures from old Christmas cards and twenty-five plain card circles of the same size.
Carefully draw the numbers 1 to 25 on the plain circles and colour them in.
Glue a picture and a number together on to the end of each pencil.

As each day of December passes, twist the pencils round to let the Christmas pictures show, and count the days left to Christmas.

14

Norway's Christmas Gift

Every year since 1947 the people of Oslo have given a Christmas tree to the city of Westminster. The gift is an expression of goodwill and gratitude for Britain's help to Norway during the 1939–45 war.

The tree is a Norwegian spruce. It is selected in late November and presented to the Lord Mayor of London who goes to Oslo to receive it.

Once the tree is cut down, it is shipped to Felixstowe and is then taken by road to London. It is erected in Trafalgar Square, where it is trimmed and dressed in Norwegian-style white lights. A crèche is set up at the foot of the tree, and, each evening until Twelfth Night, a carol service is held in the Square.

Saint Nicholas

Saint Nicholas is one of the best-loved of all the saints. During his lifetime he became so famous for his generosity and kindness that it is no wonder he became linked with Christmas.

Nicholas, who was born in Asia Minor at the end of the third century, was the only son of very wealthy parents. When he was still a boy, both his parents died leaving him in possession of a vast fortune.

Nicholas was determined to dedicate his life to the service of God and use his considerable wealth to help others.

He went to live in Myra, the capital city of Lycia, where, under extraordinary circumstances, he became a Bishop while he was still only a youth. The young Bishop devoted himself to his work, and there are many stories of his good deeds. The most famous of these is a legend which has a good deal to do with the origins of our present-day Santa Claus.

There was once a rich merchant who lost his entire fortune and fell on hard times. The merchant had three daughters, but because he had no money, he was unable to give them anything for a dowry, and without a dowry none of his girls could get married.

The family grew poorer and poorer. The merchant became ill with the worry and disgrace of not being able to provide for his daughters.

One morning, when the eldest daughter went to light the fire, she discovered a bag of gold in one of her stockings which she had hung up to dry the night before. The girl was overjoyed, and not long afterwards she married well.

When the time came for the second daughter to marry the same thing happened—a bag of gold was found in her stocking by the fireplace, and so she too was able to marry.

When the third girl was grown up her father was determined to find out who was helping them. He kept a close watch. Then one night he caught the Bishop in the very act of throwing a

bag of gold down the chimney....

Nicholas, who liked to do good secretly, begged the man not to tell anyone. But the merchant did so, and everyone learned of the Bishop's generosity.

On another occasion an innkeeper, who was an evil man, robbed and murdered some children and hid their bodies in casks of salted water. Nicholas happened to stop at the inn one night. In a dream he learned of the innkeeper's terrible crime. He made the man confess and then, after praying to God, the good Bishop miraculously restored the children to life.

Saint Nicholas is patron saint of many other people besides children. Sailors, in particular, regard him as their saint. Once when he was returning from the Holy Land by sea, a violent storm arose and the ship was in danger of sinking. Nicholas calmly prayed to God and the storm abated. It is said that during terrible storms, sailors sometimes see a vision of Saint Nicholas.

In Holland, 6 December, Saint Nicholas Day, is especially exciting for children. The Dutch people hold celebrations in honour of the saint. Dutch sailors were the first to bring back stories about his good deeds, and the people of Holland have taken the kindly Bishop to their hearts. Saint Nicholas is the patron saint of Amsterdam.

Dutch children are told that Saint Nicholas (or Sinterklaas) lives in Spain. During the year, with the help of his servant, Black Peter (or Zwarte Piet), he records the behaviour of all the children in a big red book. Then, in mid-November, he sets out by sea to arrive in Holland in time for Saint Nicholas Day.

On 6 December, children eagerly wait on the quayside of Amsterdam Harbour, and in many other of Holland's harbour cities, for Sinterklaas to appear. They sing the Saint Nicholas song:

> Look, there is a steamer from far-away
>   lands,
> It brings us Saint Nicholas, he's waving
>   his hands.
> His horse is a-prancing on deck, up and
>   down;
> The banners are waving in village and
>   town.

At last, Sinterklaas, dressed in his red bishop's cloak with mitre, jewelled gloves and crozier, and mounted on a white horse, rides majestically down the gang-plank and on through the streets. Alongside him, runs Zwarte Piet, dressed in doublet and velvet breeches and with a plumed hat. He carries a sack of presents over his shoulder and a stick with which to beat any naughty children.

Then Sinterklaas and Zwarte Piet are said to ride across over the roof-tops of Holland, leaving presents for children who put their clogs or shoes near the fireside, filled with hay and carrots for the horse. During the night, the hay and carrots are changed for presents and sweets.

Dutch people have a great deal of fun on Saint Nicholas Day hiding presents for the children to find, or making up guessing games or poems which have to be read before the present can be opened.

17

Santa Claus

When Dutch settlers arrived in New York (once called New Amsterdam), they brought with them their traditions of Saint Nicholas. On one of the early ships that came across from Holland was a carved figure representing the saint. Instead of wearing long robes and bishop's mitre, the figure was dressed in breeches and had on a wide-brimmed hat. He was also smoking a long Dutch pipe.

Settlers from other countries were fascinated by Saint Nicholas and by the festivities the Dutch people held in his honour on 6 December.

Children tried to pronounce the Dutch name for the saint—Sinter Klaas.

Gradually the saintly bishop took on a new form. He was described as being a jolly, chubby fellow driving across the sky on a sleigh pulled by reindeer. In 1822 Clement C Moore's poem 'A Visit from Saint Nicholas' gave the saint all the characteristics we associated with Santa Claus.

Finally, a picture by Thomas Nast in Harper's magazine in 1863 portrayed Santa Claus as the old gentleman with red robe and white beard that everyone recognizes today.

from 'A visit from Saint Nicholas'

And then in a twinkling I heard on the roof
The prancing and pawing of each little hoof.
As I drew in my head, and was turning around,
Down the chimney Saint Nicholas came with a bound.
He was dressed all in fur from his head to his foot,
And his clothes were all tarnished with ashes and soot;
A bundle of toys he had flung on his back,
And he looked like a peddler just opening his pack.
His eyes how they twinkled! his dimples how merry!
His cheeks were like roses, his nose like a cherry;
His droll little mouth was drawn up like a bow,
And the beard on his chin was as white as the snow.
The stump of a pipe he held tight in his teeth,
And the smoke it encircled his head like a wreath.
He had a broad face and a round little belly
That shook, when he laughed, like a bowl full of jelly.
He was chubby and plump,—a right jolly old elf,
And I laughed, when I saw him, in spite of myself.
A wink of his eye and a twist of his head
Soon gave me to know I had nothing to dread.
He spoke not a word, but went straight to his work,
And filled all the stockings; then turned with a jerk,
And laying his finger aside of his nose,
And giving a nod, up the chimney he rose.
He sprang to his sleigh, to his team gave a whistle,
And away they all flew like the down of a thistle;
But I heard him exclaim ere he drove out of sight,
'Happy Christmas to all, and to all a good-night!'

A Day in my Life

It's all go in these big shops, I can tell you. Hardly any time for a nice cup of tea. And the things those children ask for — you'd never believe it. And when I've finished I've got to go flying around in my sleigh, haven't I? And get down all those rotten chimneys again. Still it's all worth it isn't it? Isn't it?

The Real True Father Christmas

One December a little girl went shopping with her mother in a large department store. In the toy department a sort of cave had been constructed. On the outside of it there was a notice saying Father Christmas's Grotto and giving the price of admission. The main inducement to enter was the promise that every visitor would receive a gift from Father Christmas.

'Do you want to visit Father Christmas's Grotto?' asked the little girl's mother.

'Not particularly,' said the little girl.

'Well, I think you'd better,' said the mother. 'I've a few things to buy I don't want you to see. When you've finished inside, go to that stall where they were demonstrating atomic submarines and I'll join you there.'

The mother paid the price of admission and the little girl entered the grotto. Her reluctance do to so in the first place was not because she was blasé; rather that she felt it would be embarrassing to meet a fraud—a dressed-up man masquerading as Father Christmas. He would be putting on an act and she would have to put on an act as well; in other words, pretend that she thought he really was Father Christmas.

It was not even as though she believed that somewhere there was a true Father Christmas whom the man in the grotto was pretending to be; she knew very well—she had known for two or three years— that Father Christmas was an invention of parents to give their children pleasure at Christmas time. Moreover, her mother knew that she knew, so being sent out of the way via the grotto was somehow a rather humiliating way of being sent out of the way—as though she were still aged about four.

Also, she was the only patron going into the grotto, and that made her self-conscious. Perhaps at this time of day there were fewer people in the department or the admission to the grotto was priced too high or its reputation had become notorious—rotten presents, say, or a feeble Father Christmas whose beard didn't fit properly.

The entrance to the grotto was both deserted and gloomy. For some reason a battered effigy of Micky Mouse stood against one of the canvas walls: no doubt it was disinterred from the store's cellars for any occasion in which children were involved. A hidden loudspeaker of poor quality was playing Christmas carols. The canvas walls made a right-angled turn leading to a small quite gloomy open space where a figure in red robes sat in a sleigh, also of battered appearance. Some greyish icicles hung from the ceiling. What a grotty grotto, thought the little girl.

'Come along, my dear,' said the red-robed figure through his white beard and moustache. 'Don't be shy.'

There were no other visitors in this inner sanctum either. There was a little stool by the sleigh, to which the Father Christmas figure pointed his red sleeve (from which an ordinary shirt cuff protruded).

'Sit down here, there's a good girl,' he said. 'Now, what's your name, my angel?'

'Arabella Tomkins.'

'What a lovely name!' said Father Christmas.

'Do you think so?'

'I certainly do.'

'I think it's a silly name,' said Arabella.

'Good gracious, you mustn't say that,' exclaimed Father Christmas.

'Why not?'

'Well it's your name, isn't it? You've got to go through life with it and—'

'Not if I marry,' said Arabella.

'No, I see that.'

'Not that that would be much help, since Arabella's the sillier part.'

'Oh that's what you think, is it?'

'Don't you?'

'I'm not here to think,' said Father Christmas. 'I'm here to get on rapidly with my job, which is to ask you what you want me to bring you for Christmas and also to give you a gift out of this 'ere bag.'

'Why do you say "This ere bag" in that different voice?'

'Because I'm a humorous fellow,' said Father Christmas. 'Come on now, Arabella Tomkins, let's get it over with. What shall I drop down your chimney on the twenty-fourth? Doll, doll's cradle, toy trombone?'

'I think we could skip all that and get on right away with the gift part of your job,' said Arabella. 'You see I know you couldn't be Father Christmas, even if Father Christmas ever really existed.'

'I say, you pitch it a bit strong, don't you?'

'Well what I say is true, isn't it?'

Father Christmas didn't speak for a full ten seconds. Then slowly he said: 'No, it is not. What is true is that up and down the country and all over the world at this time of year there are a lot of people dressed up as Father Christmas. On Christmas Eve the number probably goes up. The supply is regulated by the demand in accordance with economic law. Obviously I couldn't be here and also at Selfridges. But that doesn't mean that somewhere there isn't a real true Father Christmas. Do you follow me?'

'Yes,' said Arabella, 'but—'

'On Christmas Eve,' continued Father Christmas, 'the part of Father Christmas is usually played by the father of the family. Father Christmases in the street—selling cheap mechanical toys, say, or advertising restaurants' Christmas dinners—are ordinary street-traders or sandwich-board men just dressed up for the seasonal occasion. Father Christmases in the better stores—I'm sure the one at Selfridges, for instance—are, more likely than not, unemployed actors, a very talented and respectable class of men. But among all those Father Christmases is the one veritable, old, original Father Christmas.'

'And do you mean to say,' said Arabella in sarcastic tones, 'that he rides on a sleigh and is pulled by reindeer and—'

'Yes I do, and he does.'

Arabella laughed.

'What is more,' said Father Christmas, extremely seriously, 'I am him. Or should it be "I am he"? Anyway, I am the real Father Christmas. You may go on sniggering, Arabella, but that can't affect the truth of the matter, which is that by a strange chance—one which may never occur again—you have met the one right, regular Father Christmas out of thousands of necessary imitations. Feel my hands.'

Arabella did so.

'You see,' said Father Christmas. 'They're cold; cold as the Prussian plains I come from. You think my whiskers are false, don't you? Pull them.'

Arabella reached out and pulled the white beard. Father Christmas uttered a slight 'ouch' and the beard remained fast.

'One final proof of my identity, if further proof were needed. I know without your telling me what you would most dearly like for Christmas, Arabella Tomkins, and I hereby solemnly promise to bring it to you. When you open the parcel on Christmas morning and find your heart's desire, remember this one moment and me, the old, original Father Christmas, who (or should it be "whom"?) you once doubted.'

Father Christmas's tones had become quite deep and tragic, and he put a bent forefinger quickly to each eye in turn, probably to dam back a starting tear.

Then he said: 'I think I hear someone else coming along. Up you get, Arabella, and on your way. Here is your somewhat miserable interim present.'

He fished about in his sack and brought out an oblong package wrapped in purple tissue paper. 'This is not my choice, of course—and I'm sure it won't be yours. It's just one of the limited selection provided by the management as advertised at the entrance and included in the price of admission to this 'ere grotto. Goodbye. Happy Christmas.'

'Happy Christmas,' said Arabella faintly, rather overcome by Father Christmas's eloquence. She walked out of the grotto. Just before the exit stood a down-at-heel representation of Donald Duck.

Arabella said nothing to her mother about her conversation with Father Christmas. The purple tissue-wrapped package proved to be the game of snakes and ladders, two versions of which she already possessed. But she had not previously possessed the main present she found in her pillowslip on her bed on Christmas morning—and which was indeed, as Father Christmas had prophesied, the thing she wanted most. How had he done it? The fact was he *had* done it, but did that make him the real Father Christmas? Arabella looked at her present, and wondered.

Make this Father Christmas

This Father Christmas could be used for a table or shelf decoration, or with a thread looped through the tip of his hat, he could hang from the Christmas tree. You will find a colour photograph of him on pp 34—5.

On pages 156—7 you will find the templates for tracing on to card or construction paper. (Remember to fold your card before you draw the outline of the legs, so that you cut it twice as long.)

If you have coloured card, then cut the following in red:
   the body, arms, hat and nose;
the following in black:
   the legs, eyes, mouth, hands, and feet;
the following in white:
   the head, beard, and moustache.

To make the figure:
   Glue up the sides of the four cones for the body, arms, and hat. Cut 1cm strips of cotton wool, and glue them around the bottom of each cone. The hat cone should have a small cotton wool ball on its tip.

Flatten the tips of the two sleeve cones slightly, and glue them to the back of the body cone. (Make sure to keep the seam where you have glued the cones to the back.) Glue the hands inside the sleeves (Fig 1).

Cut the beard into hairs and curl the ends up around a cocktail stick (Fig 2). Cut the moustache hairs and curl slightly on the ends.

The rectangle for the head has two dotted guidelines. The middle strip will be the face.

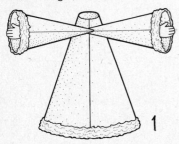

1

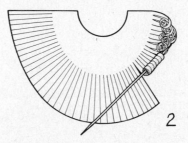

2

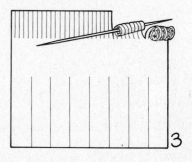

3

24

Look at Fig 3 and make short cuts for the hair. Roll these forward as you did with the beard. Make wider cuts along the bottom, then glue the head-shape into a cylinder. Squash the cuts at the bottom together to form the neck. Then, holding the head in one hand, put glue on the squashed neck pieces, and carefully push through the neck-opening of the body cone. Put your hand inside the body cone, and press the glued neck pieces on to the inside of the body. Hold until the head is firm.

The nose should be made into a squat cone by overlapping the cut in the small circle and then gluing (Fig 6). Put glue along the bottom and set in place (Fig 7). Glue on the eyes and then the hat.

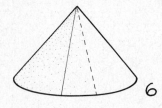

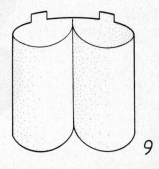

When this is dry put glue along the bottom edge and attach the feet.

Fold out the four flaps at the top of the legs and put glue on them. Then press the body cone down on to the legs. Hold in place until the glue sets.

Note: if you have only white card it will be easier to paint the various pieces in the right colours and allow them to dry before you start assembling the figure.

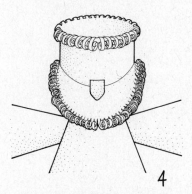

Put the mouth in place (Fig 4) and glue the moustache on top (Fig 5). (You could use the cotton wool for the beard and moustache if it seems easier.)

Cut the legs out to be double the length of the template. Glue the leg strip to form the cylinder shape shown in Fig 8. Glue the centre-fold to the back seam to make a shape like the letter B (Fig 9).

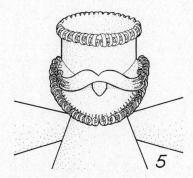

The Holly and the Ivy

Evergreens have traditionally been used to decorate the house at Christmas time, yet of all the evergreens, holly is the one which seems to represent the season of Christmas most.

Its popularity began long before the birth of Christ, however. For centuries it had been used in almost every country of the world as decoration during the midwinter festivals, when green branches were brought indoors as a magical rite to ensure the coming of spring.

It is easy to see why evergreens such as holly were once considered to be so important. Almost everything in nature withers and dies during the winter months, yet evergreens flourish and bear fruit. In early times, people believed this was because all growing things had their own spirit, and that during the winter, evergreen plants were the only ones whose spirits did not leave them.

With its handsome, shining leaves and bright red berries it is no wonder that holly was widely used as a symbol of the return of vegetation after the long months of winter.

During the festival of Saturnalia, the Romans used holly not only to decorate their homes and temples but also as a lucky token. They would exchange sprigs or sprays of it as a mark of undying friendship and as a token of good fortune and blessing for the year ahead.

As Christianity spread, many of the pagan customs continued but they were given new meanings to fit in with the new beliefs. Holly gradually became associated with the Christmas story.

One legend tells how, after the Holy Birth, the shepherds, who went to visit the Babe in the stable at Bethlehem, left behind a lamb. To keep it safe and to protect it from wolves, they put the lamb in a pen made of sharp thorn branches. But the lamb was determined to follow them, and forced its way through the thorns which cut and tore its coat. As it was a cold night, the drops of blood froze on the thorns, and this is why holly has bright red berries.

It is more widely thought that holly came to represent the crown of thorns worn by Christ at His crucifixion. In the legend, the berries of the holly were once white, but when the crown of thorns was pressed on Christ's head all holly berries turned red to represent His blood. In Denmark, the name for holly is the Christ-thorn.

People used to believe that holly brought good luck. Animals were thought to thrive if a piece was hung in the cowshed on Christmas Eve, and a holly tree planted outside the house kept it safe from lightning and fire.

Traditionally, holly and ivy go together, and they were once thought of as male and female. The prickly holly with its tough leaves was masculine and represented men. Ivy, a gentler plant of clinging habits was feminine and represented women.

When both were used to decorate the house, they would bring a happy family life for the year

to come. It was important not to bring them into the house before Christmas Eve or bad luck would follow. After Twelfth Night they would be taken down and burned, with all the other evergreen decorations.

Whichever was brought inside the house first would show whether the husband or the wife would rule the household that year. In some places, the man only would gather the holly and he would make sure it came into the house before the ivy!

An old story about the mastery of holly or ivy tells how an English lord once invited all his tenants to dine with him at Christmas. The men sat at a table decked with holly, and the women sat at one decorated with ivy. Before the meal began, the lord stood up and said to the men, 'Before you eat, let him among you who is master of his wife stand and sing us all a carol.' After a time one timid man rose to his feet and sang a short verse. The lord then turned to the women's table. 'Ivy,' he called, 'it is your turn.

Whichever one of you is master of your husband, now stand and show it by singing a carol.'

At once all the women jumped to their feet and sang so loudly that 'there was never heard such a caterwauling piece of music'. The lord laughed and called out merrily, 'I declare that the ivy is the master!'

Holly and ivy had a great quarrel,
Who should have mastery
    In land where they go.
Then spake holly: 'I am fresh and jolly,
I will have mastery
    In lands where we go.'
Then spake ivy: 'I am loud and proud,
And I will have mastery
    In lands where we go.'
Then spake holly, and kneeled on his knee.
'I pray thee gentle ivy, say nothing ill of me
    In land where we go.'

Joseph and the Cherry Tree

The legend of Joseph and the cherry tree goes back for more than five hundred years. It tells how Joseph as an old man is walking in a cherry grove with his young bride. When she describes her visits from the angel, telling her she is to bear the Holy Child, Joseph becomes angry and suspicious and refuses to pick Mary any of the cherries. He is filled with remorse when the branches of the tree bend over graciously for his young wife to pick the cherries for herself.

Joseph was an old man, and an old man was he,
When he wedded Mary, in the land of Galilee.
When Joseph and Mary walked in the garden good,
There were cherries and berries as red as the blood.

O then bespoke Mary, so meek and so mild;
'Pluck me some cherries, Joseph, for I am with child.'
O then bespoke Joseph, with words so unkind;
'Let him pluck the cherries that brought thee with child.'

O then bespoke Jesus in his mother's womb:
'Bow down then, the tallest tree, that my mother may have some.'
Then bowed down the tallest tree, it bent to Mary's hand.
Then she cried, 'See, Joseph, I have cherries at command.'

O then bespoke Joseph; 'I have done Mary wrong.
But cheer up, my dearest, and be not cast down.'
Then Joseph and Mary did to Bethlehem go
And with travels were weary walking to and fro.

They sought for a lodging, but the inns were fill'd all,
They, alas! could not have it, but in an ox's stall.
But before the next morning, Our Saviour was born,
In the month of December, Christmas Day in the morn.

Albert's Christmas Ship

Below the military striking clock in the City Arcade there was, and for all I know still is, a fabulous toyshop, the nearest thing on earth to Santa's workshop.

Once a year, at Christmas time, everybody who was anybody was taken to see the clock strike noon—an event in our lives as colourful and as regular as, say, the Trooping of the Colour.

Even Albert Skinner, whose father never took him anywhere, not even to the Education Office to explain why he'd been playing truant from school, somehow tagged on like a stray dog. And after the clock had chimed, and the mechanical soldiers and the king had trundled back into their plaster garrison, Albert, like the rest of us, was allowed to press his nose to the toyshop window and gaze inside in wonder and envy.

After this, we were taken home on the rattling tram; and once there, thawing out our frozen legs by the fireside, we were supposed to write our letters to Father Christmas.

With blank sheets of paper on our knees, we would suck our copying pencils until our tongues turned purple. It wasn't that we were short of ideas. Far from it; there was too much choice. For the fabulous toyshop was a place of dreams and of longings. There was the big clockwork train and a small electric train, and Noah's Ark, and a tram conductor's set, and a fairy cycle, and a tin steam-roller, and annuals, and board games, and chemistry sets, and conjuring sets. And for the centrepiece of the window display there was always something special: the Blackpool Tower in Meccano, or a mechanical carousel with horses that went up and down on their brass poles, or Windsor Castle made of a million building bricks.

This year the window featured a splendid model of the *Queen Mary*, which had not long been launched on Clydebank. It was about four feet long, with real lights in the portholes, real steam curling out of the funnels, and passengers and lifeboats, all to scale—and clearly it was not for the likes of us.

Having marvelled at it, we dismissed this expensive dream from our minds and settled down to list our more ordinary requests for Plasticene, farmyard animals that poisoned you when you licked the paint off, or one pair of roller-skates between the pair of us.

All of us, that is except Albert Skinner, who calmly announced that he was asking Father Christmas for the *Queen Mary*. This, as you might imagine, was greeted with some scepticism.

'You've never asked for that, have you? You're having us on.'

'I'm not—God's honour.'

'What else did you ask for?'

'Nowt. I don't want owt else. I just want the *Queen Mary*. And I'm getting it as well.'

Little else was said at the time, but privately we thought Albert was a bit of an optimist. For one thing, the *Queen Mary* was so big and so grand and so lit-up that it was probably not even for sale. For another, we were well aware that Albert's father was a grumpy bad-tempered man who happened to be unemployed. Albert's birthday present, it was generally known, had been a pair of boots—instead of the scooter on which he had set his heart.

Even so, Albert continued to insist that he was getting the *Queen Mary* for Christmas. 'Ask my dad,' he would say. 'If you don't believe me, ask my dad.'

None of us cared to broach the subject with the moody Mr Skinner. But sometimes, when we went to swap comics, Albert would raise the matter himself. 'Dad, I am, aren't I? Getting that *Queen*

Mary for Christmas?'

Mr Skinner, dourly whittling a piece of wood by the fireside after the habit of all the local miners, would growl without looking up: 'You'll get a clout over the bloomin' earhole if you don't stop nattering.'

Albert would turn to us complacently. 'I am, see. I'm getting the *Queen Mary*.'

Sometimes, when his father had come home from the pub in a bad mood, which was quite often, Albert's pleas would meet with a more vicious response. 'Will you shut up about the *Queen Mary*!' Mr Skinner would shout. 'If I hear one more word about it, you'll get nothing for Christmas!'

Outside, his ear tingling from the blow his father had landed on it, Albert would bite back the tears and declare stubbornly: 'I am still getting it. You just wait.'

Then one day the crippled lad at No 43 was taken to see the military striking clock, and when he came home he reported that the *Queen Mary* was no longer in the toyshop window. 'I know,' said Albert, having confirmed that his father was out of earshot. 'I'm getting it for Christmas.'

And, indeed, it seemed the only explanation possible. The fabulous toyshop never changed its glittering display until after Boxing Day—never. And yet the *Queen Mary* had gone. Had Father Christmas gone mad? Had Mr Skinner bribed him—and if so, with what? Had Mr Skinner won the football pools? Or was it that Albert's unswerving faith could move mountains—not to mention ocean-going liners with real steam and real lights in the portholes.

'You just wait and see,' said Albert.

Then it was Christmas morning, and we all flocked out to show off our presents, sucking our brand-new torches to make our cheeks glow red, or brandishing a lead soldier or two in the pretence that we had a whole regiment of them indoors.

There was no sign of Albert. No one, in fact, expected to see him at all. But just as we were asking each other what Father Christmas could have brought him—a new jersey perhaps, or a balaclava helmet—he came bounding, leaping, almost somersaulting into the street. 'I've got it! I've got it!'

Toys and games abandoned in the gutter, we clustered round Albert, who was cradling in his arms what seemed on first inspection to be a length of wood. Then we saw that it had been carved at both ends to make a bow and stern, and that three cotton reels had been nailed to it for funnels. A row of tin-tacks marked the plimsoll line, and there were stuck-on bits of cardboard for the portholes. The whole thing was painted in sticky lamp-black, except for the wobbling white lettering on the port side. 'ThE QuEEn MaRy' it said.

'See!' crowed Albert, complacently. 'I told you he'd fetch me it, and he's fetched me it.'

Our grunts of appreciation were real enough. Albert's *Queen Mary* was a crude piece of work, but clearly many hours of labour, and much love, had gone into it. Its clumsy contours alone must have taken night after night of whittling by the fireside.

Mr Skinner, pyjama-jacket tucked into his trousers, had come out of the house and was standing by his garden gate. Albert, in a rush of happiness, flung his arms round his father and hugged him. Then he held the *Queen Mary* on high.

'Look, Dad! Look what Father Christmas has fetched me. You knew he would, didn't you, all the time!'

'Get out of it, you soft little beggar,' said Mr Skinner, cuffing Albert over the head as a matter of habit before going indoors.

The Poinsettia—Flower of the Holy Night

It is the Mexicans who call the poinsettia 'Flower of the Holy Night'; and the Holy Night is the Mexican way of saying 'Christmas Eve'.

Legend tells us that the whole thing started in a place called Cuernavaca where, one Christmas Eve, a little peasant girl was standing outside the great doors of the cathedral. She watched sadly as well-to-do families and rich, haughty women hurried in to mass, carrying with them gifts as offerings to the Christ Child.

The little peasant girl longed to be able to take a gift of her own into the cathedral, so that she too could make an offering. But she had nothing to give because she was so poor. Then an angel appeared to her, telling her to pick some of the tall wild plants which grew at the roadside.

Joyfully the little girl carried the spindly plants inside and made her way to the altar where the gifts were being received. But the people looked at her in dismay. The haughty women threw up their hands in horror. Some of the children sniggered: 'Look at her, bringing weeds into the church!' A priest hurried up as if to hustle the little girl outside. Her cheeks burned crimson with shame, and her eyes brimmed with tears as she turned to hurry out of the cathedral.

Suddenly, the topmost leaves on each stem of the plant became a wonderful and radiant red, as if it had burst into flame. The people were amazed, and some of them fell to their knees as the child proudly carried her 'fire flowers' to the altar.

Incredible as it sounds, this amazing plant has a built-in time switch, and if you do things right, you can get its top leaves to burst into flame-coloured red, actually, any time you like.

The secret behind the miracle is that the poinsettia is photo-periodic or light-sensitive. Its growth varies according to the amount of light it gets. If a healthy, mature plant is given 11 hours of light each day continuously for 70 days, at the

end of that time it will suddenly and dramatically burst into bloom.

In this country and in America the poinsettia is called after the man who introduced it to the world at large, in 1836. He was called Dr Joel Poinsett and, as well as being a keen botanist, was the first United States Ambassador to Mexico.

The plants which amazed Joel Poinsett, all those years ago were tall, rather spindly things; not really very much like the beautiful, highly cultivated ones we now see everywhere at Christmas decorating greetings cards and gift labels, and as a motif on wrapping paper. And, of course, as gifts for the home. Dr Poinsett's original plants grew in the jungle, where conditions were exactly right for the upper leaves to burst into brilliant red just before Christmas. Gradually, people got the idea of collecting them and selling them as decorations for the home at Christmas time.

Things to Make

Here are some photographs of things you can make from this book. You will find the Advent Calendar on p. 14, Father Christmas on p. 24, Christmas cards p. 38, the Kissing Bush p. 58, the Snowman p. 66, the Mexican Piñata p. 80, the Choir of Angels p. 104, egg decorations p. 114 the edible decorations p. 122, and the Crèche p. 12.

Christmas Cards

Before there were postmen, how did people send Christmas greetings? The answer is that few people ever did. Of course letters, written notes, and little hand-drawn pictures had for a long time been exchanged at Christmas.

In the eighteenth century, children were made to copy out a carefully worded letter called a 'Christmas piece' in their very best copper-plate handwriting. The 'piece' wished their parents the compliments of the season. The neatness and care taken by the children was meant to show how they were progressing.

Beautiful hand-illuminated texts had, for centuries, been prepared by monks to mark important religious festivals.

Well-to-do ladies with time to spare might paint little designs or pictures with a seasonal theme in watercolours to give to their acquaintances.

When the Penny Post was started in 1840 it became much easier for people to send greetings to their friends.

Then in 1843, a well-known man-about-town, too busy for writing letters, asked an artist friend to design a card for him with a printed message which he could just sign. A thousand copies of the card were produced, and the very first Christmas card as we know it came into being.

The man was Henry Cole, director of London's famous Victoria and Albert Museum. His card, which was designed by Ralph C Horsley had three panels: a large central one shows merrymakers giving a toast; the other two panels depict the hungry being fed and the poor being clothed.

But it was not until the late 1860s that the practice of sending Christmas cards became really widespread. Until then, one popular way of sending greetings had been to write a letter on notepaper printed with decorated borders, showing such seasonal items as sprays of holly, mistletoe, robins, and hampers.

By 1870 the Christmas card boom had begun: the halfpenny post was introduced for cards in unsealed envelopes, and the cards themselves had become cheaper because of new methods of colour printing.

In fact Christmas cards became so successful that even in 1880 the Postmaster General was having to warn everybody to 'post early for Christmas'!

Using the profit from the sale of cards for charity was the idea of Dr Wilfred Grenfell. In 1912 he wanted to raise money for the Eskimos and Indians in his missions in Newfoundland and Labrador. This card was designed by Dr Grenfell (later Sir Wilfred Grenfell) himself in 1929.

One of the biggest charities to gain from the sale of cards has been the United Nations' Children's Organization, UNICEF. Its first card, produced in 1949, was drawn by a seven-year-old Czechoslovakian girl called Jitka Samkova.

A HAPPY XMAS.

Santa Claus in Labrador.

Cheero!

TO
BLIGHTY·AND·YOU

A soldier's Christmas card from the First World War (1914–18).

A Victorian Christmas card showing a street scene.

UNICEF

MR PUNCH

WISHES YOU
A MERRY
CHRISTMAS
AND A
HAPPY NEW YEAR

Make your own Christmas Cards

To make the Christmas Cards you will need:
scissors,
paper paste,
latex glue,
a paper punch (if you have one),
sharp pencil and ruler,
thin white or coloured card.
Look around and see what items you can collect together to make a 'workbox' of odds and ends.

You can use such items as:
unusual buttons and beads,
seeds, sequins,
ribbon, lace, piping cord,
wool, scraps of vilene,
paper doileys,
textured paper,
sugar paste, tissue paper,
old gift-wrapping paper,
gummed stars, spots and shapes.

To make the cards
Use the templates at the front and back of the book. Trace them on to card and cut out of your card one of the shapes you want to use.

Start by decorating the shape as your central figure. Use your imagination. For example, you can cut out simple shapes like stripes, circles and triangles. Dots can be made with a paper punch or can be bought at a stationers.
Where you want fur or snow, scraps of vilene left over from dressmaking are most useful. More exotic effects come with the use of metallic suede or fluorescent papers, or self-adhesive tape.

Tissue paper comes in lovely colours. A good tip when cutting it out is to iron the piece on to the shiny side of iron-on vilene before you cut it out.

Cut out your card to suit the decorated shape. You can vary the shape and size as you think best. Try making round cards for round compositions (Fig 1).

For contrast, a panel of coloured paper can be glued to the front of the card. If you have any self-adhesive gift-wrapping ribbon

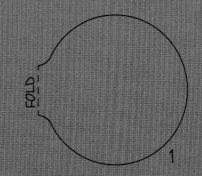

FOLD

1

you can put strips of this round your picture to make a frame.

To achieve a 'standing out' effect, add mice heads made from vilene and give them lurex whiskers (Fig 2).

To make the 'partridge in the pear tree', fold the card in half and then fold half the front so that it stands back on itself (Fig 3). Cut out tree shape and glue on leaves. Paste the tree on to the front half of the folded panel, so

that when it stands up it will cast shadows on the back page of the card (Fig 4).
Make the partridge stand out by making a small box-shape (Fig 5) to glue behind the bird before you glue it on to the tree.

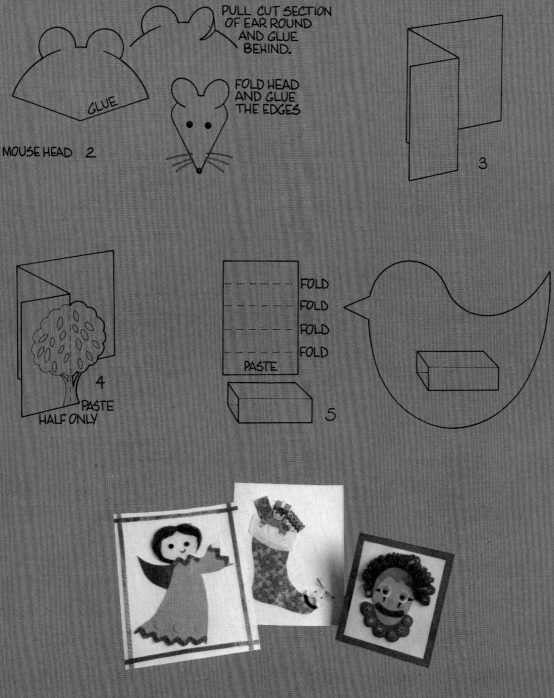

PULL CUT SECTION OF EAR ROUND AND GLUE BEHIND.

FOLD HEAD AND GLUE THE EDGES

GLUE

MOUSE HEAD 2

3

4
PASTE HALF ONLY

FOLD
FOLD
FOLD
FOLD
PASTE

5

The Twelve Days of Christmas

The first day of Christmas
My true love sent to me.
A partridge in a pear-tree.

The second day of Christmas
My true love sent to me
Two turtle-doves
And a partridge in a pear-tree.

The third day of Christmas
My true love sent to me
Three French hens,
Two turtle-doves
And a partridge in a pear-tree.

The fourth day of Christmas
My true love sent to me
Four colly birds,
Three French hens,
Two turtle-doves
And a partridge in a pear-tree.

The fifth day of Christmas
My true love sent to me
Five gold rings,
Four colly birds,
Three French hens,
Two turtle-doves
And a partridge in a pear-tree.

The sixth day of Christmas
My true love sent to me
Six geese a-laying,
Five gold rings,
Etc.

The seventh day of Christmas
My true love sent to me
Seven swans a-swimming,
Etc.

The eighth day of Christmas
My true love sent to me
Eight maids a-milking,
Etc.

The ninth day of Christmas
My true love sent to me
Nine drummers drumming,
Etc.

The tenth day of Christmas
My true love sent to me
Ten pipers piping,
Etc.

The eleventh day of Christmas
My true love sent to me
Eleven ladies dancing,
Etc.

The twelfth day of Christmas
My true love sent to me
Twelve lords a-leaping,
Eleven ladies dancing,
Ten pipers piping,
Nine drummers drumming,
Eight maids a-milking,
Seven swans a-swimming,
Six geese a-laying,
Five gold rings,
Four colly birds,
Three French hens,
Two turtle-doves
And a partridge in a pear-tree.

The Man who went 'Crackers' at Christmas

When Tom Smith used a novel form of packaging in the 1840s, he didn't realize he had 'invented' a tradition that would become a part of Christmas the world over.

Everyone loves to pull a cracker. It's all part of the fun of Christmas. The originator of the cracker was a man called Tom Smith who owned a sweet shop in London.

Tom had a good eye for business. He also had a sense of humour. 'What people like,' he used to say, 'is something *new*. And if it's *not* new, the art is to find a way of selling it!'

During the 1840s Tom found that people liked sugar almonds, but while he was on holiday in France he came across a variety of sweets wrapped up in a twist of paper. These bonbons seemed very popular, so Tom decided to copy the idea to wrap his sugar almonds.

The new wrapping made the sweets look rather special. They sold well. Then Tom noticed that young men were buying them to give to their sweethearts. He began placing 'love mottoes' on small slips of paper inside the sweet wrapping.

This novelty sold even better than Tom had expected. People went out of their way to visit his shop and buy this new kind of sweet.

In 1846 Tom turned his thoughts towards Christmas. Instead of sweets, why not wrap little toys and novelties in the twisted wrapping? Tom experimented and hit on the idea of producing a wrapping that could be pulled apart—just like the cracker as we know it today.

As he had hoped, the Christmas novelty was a success, but Tom was still not satisfied. One evening he was standing idly in front of the fire. As he kicked a log into place there was a shower of sparks and the log crackled and popped, making Tom jump.

'That's it!' he laughed to himself. 'What I need is something in my wrapping that will make a "snap" when it is pulled open. That would be fun at Christmas time.'

For some months he worked with several chemicals until at last he found one that was safe, easy to make, and would make a noise just loud enough to amuse his customers and not frighten them.

The new 'crackers' were a sensation, and soon making them became a full-time business. Tom had to open a factory to produce them.

Today the Tom Smith factory sells crackers all over the world, and the man who liked to amuse his customers would be amazed to know that his sense of fun had started a Christmas tradition.

The big pictures show Tom Smith's
original crackers. The little pictures show
modern-day crackers.

Why do we Kiss beneath the Mistletoe?

In ancient times, the mistletoe was thought of as the plant of peace and friendship. If enemies met under a tree on which mistletoe grew, they would lay down their arms and call a truce for the rest of the day. If friends met beneath a tree bearing mistletoe, they would consider their friendship to be blessed with good luck.

Kissing under the mistletoe has come from a custom which was once found only in England. Foreign visitors to England in the sixteenth century were often surprised how often men and women exchanged kisses in greeting and in parting. Perhaps it was this practice, as well as the belief that mistletoe was a plant of friendship, that led to the Christmas tradition.

From early times, evergreens such as holly, ivy and laurel were used as Christmas decorations. A large bough of mistletoe would be picked to form the centre of a huge garland to be hung in a room or hall. Any young woman who stood beneath the garland (or kissing bough) would expect to receive a kiss. It would bring her luck and ensure her of marriage. She also had the right to pluck a berry from the mistletoe for every kiss she received. Once the sprig had no more berries, it was no longer lucky to kiss under it. After Twelfth Night, the mistletoe would be burned, otherwise the young men and women who kissed under it might never marry.

The Celtic Druids worshipped the mistletoe because it grew on their sacred tree, the oak. When the oak

leaves died in the autumn, the mistletoe stayed green. The Druids believed that the spirit of the oak passed into the mistletoe for the winter to return when new oak leaves began to form in the Spring. During the festivals of the winter and summer solstice, white-robed Druids would perform a ceremony where a bough of mistletoe would be cut with a golden sickle. The chief

Druid would not touch the mistletoe but allow it to fall into a white cloth. During the ceremony, two white oxen would be sacrificed.

Many superstitions surround the mistletoe. Like other Christmas greenery it was not to be brought into the house before 24 December, nor was it to be left up

after Twelfth Night. In some places one sprig of mistletoe would be put away to be kept all year to bring luck to the household. If a baby was born, a piece of the mistletoe would be placed in the cradle to keep the child from harm. Sometimes a sprig of mistletoe would be given to a cow that had calved to bring good luck to the herd.

An ancient name for mistletoe is 'the wood of the Holy Cross'. Mistletoe is never taken into a church at any time. This is because of a legend which tells how mistletoe wood was used to make the cross on which Christ died. Afterwards, all mistletoe shrank to its present size in shame and anguish. Mistletoe is not used to decorate a church at Christmas, although in the Middle Ages a sprig was ceremonially laid on the altar of York Minster.

The Story of the Christmas Tree

Most people think that the tradition of lighting and decorating a fir tree at Christmas time originated in Germany. Perhaps this is because so many charming ceremonies and customs to do with Christmas trees do come from Germany.

A decorated tree in the home was familiar to the Romans, who enjoyed the festival of Saturnalia. Sometimes they used to put twelve candles on the tree (one for each month of the calendar), and on the top they placed an image of Apollo, the god of the sun. They also decorated their houses with branches of bay and laurel, on which they hung trinkets and tiny masks of the god Bacchus.

In Northern Europe the Teutonic tribes used to decorate trees in honour of their chief god Odin (or Woden). They used such things as apples, and cakes made in the shape of fish, birds, or animals. These decorations were a symbol of Odin's favour towards his people.

The Druids also used to bring evergreens indoors during their winter festival, as these trees appeared 'not to die' during the winter months, unlike the others whose spirit, the Druids believed, had departed. The evergreen branches symbolized the return of life and growth in plants and trees. As Christianity spread, the winter rites continued but were changed in honour of Christ as the 'bringer of new life into the world'. In northern Europe, where there were so many forests, it was natural for the branches of the fir tree to be used as the emblem of renewal.

It was the great German reformer, Martin Luther (1483–1546) who is said to have introduced the Christmas tree as we know it, with its mass of beautiful shining lights. The story tells how, one Christmas, Luther was walking home through a forest. He was deeply moved by the beauty of the starlit sky above the dark stately fir trees. When he reached home he tried to describe the beauty of the scene to his wife and child, but unable to find words, he went out and cut a small fir tree and placed lighted candles on it. 'Look,' he said, 'this is how it was—and this is how it must have been on the night the Holy Babe was born.'

Christmas Eve in Germany. Martin Luther and his family.

Gradually the practice of decorating a tree with ornaments and lighted candles spread across northern Europe and into Scandinavia. Austria is said to have had its first tree in 1816 when Princess Henriette set one up in Vienna. In 1840 Princess Helene of Mecklenburg brought the idea to Paris. In England it had always been a custom to decorate an evergreen garland called a 'kissing bush', but in 1841 Prince Albert, Consort to Queen Victoria, introduced a tree decorated with candles, tinsel, and ornaments as part of the Christmas celebrations at Windsor Castle. After that, the Christmas tree became popular in England, too.

Robin Redbreast
The Christmas Bird

No one would ever dream of harming a robin. This cheerful bird is so friendly and trusting that it will fly on to window sills and wait for food, or even fly indoors in search of a snack during very hard winters.

Its company is particularly enjoyed by gardeners, for a robin will often perch on a spade and watch bright-eyed for worms or insects in the freshly dug earth.

Robins are not timid when it comes to building their nests. A pair once set up home in a village school piano. The children had to sing without the piano for the rest of the term while the robins hatched out their young in warmth and comfort.

When robins are born, they wear a nest camouflage of speckled brown and they resemble a small thrush. As the weeks pass, the red breast-feathers emerge until finally the breast, throat, and face become orange-red to contrast with the white stomach below.

According to legend, the robin helped mankind by bringing fire to the earth, but in doing so he scorched his breast. In another legend the robin got his red breast in the stable at Bethlehem when, to warm the Christ Child, he fanned the dying fire in a brazier until it

A Merry Christmas and a Happy New Year

glowed red hot.

Robins may well be called 'Christmas card birds'. There are thousands of greetings cards which portray the little robin in his bright red waistcoat. Robin Christmas cards were especially popular in Victorian times. Robins also featured on St Valentine's Day cards and were often shown carrying a letter in their beaks.

This may be because the very first postmen wore bright red coats from 1840 to 1861. Red had been chosen for the postmen's uniform because it was the royal colour. The uniform was changed in 1861 to blue, but it is clear that the robin-postman on the greetings cards was a reflection of the real postmen in their bright red coats.

The Best Present of All

'Emma! Emma, wake up! Get dressed and come downstairs!'

Granny Sawyer set the oil lamp down on the chest of drawers and pulled back the curtains at Emma's window. It was still dark outside. A thick frost had grown on the inside of the window panes like the fronds of a delicate fern.

'Beautiful!' thought Emma, half sitting up.

'Come on, girl,' cried Granny Sawyer. 'You'll have to set to. The fire in the range is out and the house is as cold as charity. Your mother's begun the pains. I think the baby could be starting.'

Emma sat bolt upright and stared at her grandmother. The lamp threw shadows across the old lady's sharp features. The cold in the bedroom was intense, and Emma noticed that Granny Sawyer's cheeks were blue, and her breathing was short and wheezy.

'I'll dress downstairs,' said Emma. She swung her legs out of bed. She had kept her vest on under her flannel nightdress, but during the night she had taken a pair of her long black stockings from her drawer and put them on to keep her feet warm.

The rest of her clothes were downstairs. The night before, she had hung them to keep warm over the brass fireguard which stood in front of the big black range.

Emma's brother Billy was already up, trying to light the fire. The range was the only means of heating in the house, apart from a coal fire in the parlour and one in her mother's bedroom.

On one side of the range was an oven, in the centre was the fire, and on the other side was a tank for heating water. The hot water was drawn off from a brass tap at the bottom of the tank.

When the fire was alight and glowing, the range was warm and comforting. It heated the kitchen, cooked the meals, warmed the water, dried the clothes, and drew people to sit by its cheery comforts. But when the fire was out, the range was cold, black, dirty, and malevolent. Emma often wondered if it had a mind of its own, so that it could sense a crisis and put itself out—just to be spiteful.

Billy nursed and coaxed the early stages of his fire, which would either set the coal aglow or go out completely, depending on the mood of the range. He had pushed the fireguard to one side. And now

Emma's clothes, and those of her two younger sisters, Dorothy and May, lay in an untidy pile on the floor.

'It's only half-past five,' cried Emma, struggling with the fastenings that held her thick woollen bloomers to her vest. 'Oh, why is everything so awkward when your hands are cold?'

Granny Sawyer bustled into the kitchen. 'We'll not wake May or Dorothy yet,' she said. 'I'll leave that to you, Emma. You'll have to see to the breakfast. And hurry up with that fire, Billy. Oh, I've never been so cold. It's as bitter as a workhouse down here. Your poor mother will need hot water, and we'll all need a cup of tea.'

Emma had put on her petticoat and dress. She felt chilled to the bone. She slipped her feet into her button-sided boots and reached for the button-hook that hung on the wall.

'May I go up and see mother?' she asked.

'No, you may not,' snapped Granny Sawyer. 'You're all to keep away from her. What's going on is woman's work. Now, why do you think I got up so early? Hurry down to Mrs Tickner's and tell her to come. Say that things may have started. Make haste with those boot buttons.'

Wrapped in her coat and scarf and with hat and mittens on, Emma made her way down the street to the house of Mrs Tickner, the midwife. There were no street lights and, on either side of her, the houses were dark and silent. Emma's feet, in her tight leather boots, throbbed with the cold. Her breath rose like smoke in the cold air.

There had been a light fall of snow in the night, and in the pale light of a starlit sky the trees and bushes were silvery white. Emma felt a strange still beauty all around her.

She remembered that it was 24 December. So it would be today, on Christmas Eve, that her mother's baby would be born. She had longed that it might arrive on Christmas Day, for she had heard somewhere that a baby born on that day would be blessed with good fortune.

At last she arrived at Mrs Tickner's house and knocked loudly. With surprising ease, she woke the midwife, who, being used to calls at all hours of the night, was soon ready to accompany Emma back to her house.

For Emma and Billy the early hours of the morning dragged by until at last the sky had lightened into day. The range had decided to behave itself and Emma made porridge for Dorothy and May, who were woken and called down to breakfast.

Mrs Tickner and Granny Sawyer appeared from time to time for cups of tea, and Emma was told to keep the kettle on the boil at all times.

'I want you children to be good,' Granny Sawyer told them sternly as she left the room. 'Your mother's having a bad time. You know she's been poorly. Well, the baby's in no hurry to arrive. We must just pray that everything will be all right.'

The old lady's words struck a chill through Emma. 'Everything *will* be all right won't it, Billy? With mother and the baby? I mean, what if . . .'

Dorothy sensed Emma's fears and began to cry. 'Why can't Daddy be here?' she sobbed. 'Oh, why can't he be here, Billy?'

Billy tried to smile. 'A soldier can't come home just because a baby's being born. What kind of army would it be if that happened?'

'But we wrote to him just before Granny Sawyer came. We told him how bad mother was,' cried May. 'You said father might be able to come home on compassionate leave.'

Billy looked at her. There was a frown on his face as if he didn't believe what he was going to say. 'A soldier has to do his duty to King and country. He can't always get leave to come home just because . . . well . . . he just can't.'

At that moment there was a tap on the window. It was Harry Judd the postman. 'A letter! A letter!' shouted Dorothy and May.

'It's from Ireland,' said Dorothy, excitedly. 'I can see from the stamp. It'll be from father.'

Billy took the letter and tore it open. Inside was a Christmas card, a letter for their mother in a separate envelope, and a letter for them. Billy's face fell. 'It's dated 18 December. It's only just arrived here. *We* wrote to father on the 20th telling him about mother. He probably won't have got our letter yet.'

'Read what he's written to us,' said Emma quietly.

> 3rd Battalion,
> Royal Berkshire Regiment,
> Dublin
> 18 December 1917

My Dearest Children

I send my fondest love to you all as Christmas approaches. I trust you are well and happy despite the hard times which war brings. I am thankful not to be fighting in a cold muddy trench in France this Christmas, although a soldier's life is not easy here in Ireland after all the 'troubles'.

You know I cannot be with you, so, Billy, you must be the 'man of the house'. And you, Emma, must look after your mother. Be good, Dorothy and May. I shall be home sometime in the New Year, perhaps in time for the baby's arrival. I will bring your presents when I come, for the post is so bad these days.

God bless you,
from your ever loving father.

Billy folded the letter and began to poke the fire furiously so that the others would not see the tears that were stinging his eyes. Emma sprang to her feet and began clearing away the breakfast things. She, too, couldn't let Dorothy and May see the tears that had welled into her own eyes. But it was May who gave vent to all their feelings. She drew her knees up to her chest and rocked back and forth, sobbing quietly.

'You said father would be able to come home on compassionate leave,' she said through her sobs. 'We wrote and told him how ill mother is. It's Christmas but we've got nothing. Father isn't coming. We haven't even got any presents. We've no decorations. We haven't even got anything special to eat. All we've got is Granny Sawyer and she's got no time for us.'

Billy swung round and seized May's shoulders, shaking her angrily. 'Stop it! Stop it, May,' he shouted. 'Father told you to be good. You must try to be brave. All this is nobody's fault. It's nobody's fault that we can't have a proper Christmas.'

Granny Sawyer burst into the room. 'Have you children no feelings? I can hear you squabbling even from your mother's room. Now stop it at once or I'll fetch a stick to you all.'

Emma held out the envelope addressed to their mother. 'This came. It's from father,' she said.

The old lady took the envelope from Emma and placed it on the mantelpiece. 'Your mother is in no state to read it, or to worry about anything. And for that matter, neither am I.'

Emma could see the lines of worry on her grandmother's face. How could the old lady think about providing for Christmas with so much on her mind? 'I'm sorry, Gran,' she said. 'We all are.'

The old lady's face softened. 'Mrs Tickner's leaving soon. She thinks the baby won't be born for some time yet. I want you to stay here, Emma, in case I need you. Dorothy, May, I want you to go shopping. Buy some bread and sausages, and get some potatoes. Then go off and play in the snow. Wrap up warm, mind. Billy, you'd best stay out of the way, too, but make sure there's plenty of coal in.'

For the rest of the morning, Emma stayed in the kitchen. Remembering what May had said about no Christmas decorations, she found some scraps of paper and made up some paste from flour and water and began to make some paper chains.

May and Dorothy came in later on. They were blue with cold, so Emma made them tea and sat them before the range to get warm. For lunch they had cold meat and boiled potatoes and all afternoon the three girls set to work making the paper chains that Emma had begun earlier.

Billy was nowhere to be seen. 'He's probably with his beloved rabbits,' said Dorothy. 'You know how he loves them. Sometimes I think those rabbits mean more to him than anything else.'

Emma nodded. 'He'll be with those rabbits for sure,' she said. 'But it's getting dark now. I expect he'll soon be home.'

When Billy did come home, he had with him the branch of a fir tree sticking up from a large flowerpot. 'Why look,' he cried. 'You've made paper chains and I've brought the Christmas tree. We can soon make the room look jolly.'

Emma made tea for them all, and Granny Sawyer came down and joined them. 'Your mother's sleeping just now, although she's restless enough, poor soul.'

After tea the children put up the paper chains and decorated the fir tree branch which whatever bright things they could find. Afterwards they sat round the glowing fire in the range. Then very softly, Emma started to sing a carol:

> 'Away in a manger,
> No crib for a bed,
> The little lord Jesus
> Lay down his sweet head.'

The others joined in, but after a while, Mrs Tickner came in. She was going to sit up with Granny Sawyer to look after mother all night, so Granny Sawyer sent the children to bed.

Emma lay awake in bed for a long time thinking about her mother. She remembered how pale and run-down her mother had been for the past two months until at last, just before Christmas, she had to be put to bed. Emma thought, too, of her father, who had been in Ireland since August. How she longed to see him again! She recalled the day he had left, and how they had walked across the common to the station where he was to catch the train; and how the buttercups that grew in the grass had coated her boots with a golden dust. 'One day I'll buy you a real pair of golden slippers,' her father had told her as he kissed her goodbye.

Thinking of this Emma, at last, fell asleep.

'Happy Christmas, Emma!' Billy was shaking her awake. 'Come on, get up and come downstairs. Mrs Tickner's looking after mother, and Granny's asleep. The kitchen's nice and warm. I've made the breakfast, and I've a surprise for you.'

Dorothy and May were out of bed, so together they all went down to the kitchen. 'What is it, Billy?' asked Emma.

Billy pointed to the Christmas tree. Beneath it, wrapped in coloured paper, were little presents for each of them. Dorothy and May jumped up and down with excitement.

Billy handed them the presents and they opened them. Inside Emma's was a tiny brooch and a comb. May had some hair ribbons and a tiny doll. Dorothy had a box of colouring crayons and a bar of chocolate.

'Oh Billy,' said Emma. 'Thank you! Thank you so much. They're lovely. But how could you have afforded all these things for us? You've no money!'

Then a thought struck her. Billy hadn't sold his rabbits to get the money, had he? Not his beloved rabbits that meant so much to him. He couldn't have!

But Billy had, and he sensed that Emma had guessed it, for he grasped her wrist, hurting her with the force of his grip. 'Don't say anything,' he whispered fiercely. 'Don't let on and spoil things. It's Christmas. I *wanted* to do it.'

Emma pulled Billy's face towards her and kissed his cheek. 'Thank you, Billy,' she said again.

Suddenly there was a loud cry from their mother's bedroom. It was followed by another. Mrs Tickner's voice could be heard calling out, and Granny Sawyer appeared, a rug round her shoulders, from the parlour, where she had been asleep.

'Is mother all right?' Emma called up the stairs. Mrs Tickner was still on the landing. 'I think baby has made up his mind at last,' she called down. 'Everything's all right, but you children go off and play somewhere. Come on Mrs Sawyer, there's work to be done!'

'Oh, can't we stop in the house?' pleaded Dorothy.

'No, you're best out of the way,' said Granny Sawyer. 'Now be off with you.'

Another cry, long and loud, came from their mother's bedroom. Emma hurried her sisters into warm outdoor clothes, and wrapping up warmly herself, ushered them out of the house.

Emma left Dorothy and May to play on an ice-slide they had made in the snow. And she set off towards the common to be alone.

The snow was loose and powdery. The morning was sharp and bright and beautiful. Soon Emma's boots were coated white with snow, and she remembered the day when they had been golden with the dust of the buttercups.

'Please, God, may mother and the baby be all right,' she whispered. 'And please send father home to us soon.'

In the distance, the hoot of a train broke the stillness of the morning. The train appeared, the white smoke from its funnel standing out against the clear blue sky. Emma watched the train draw closer and slow down as it approached the tiny station.

A man had pulled down his window and was reaching out to open the door; a man in soldier's uniform, with his kit-bag slung over his shoulder, ready to get off the train.

Emma stared in disbelief. 'It can't be! It can't be him.'

'Emma! Emma!' It was her father waving and calling to her.

She rushed across the snow-covered common and tumbled headlong into the station entrance and her father's waiting arms.

'Your letter arrived yesterday,' her father said after he could free himself from his daughter's hugs. 'They gave me compassionate leave straight away, and I just caught the last train and got on the very last boat across. Then I managed to catch the last night train down—and here I am!'

With her eyes shining with tears, and half laughing, half sobbing, Emma took her father's hand and they walked home across the common.

'It's been terrible for mother, but now the baby's started. That's why I was on the common. We've all been sent out of the house.'

She told him how there was nothing in the house for Christmas, and how Billy had sold his rabbits to buy presents for them.

'But didn't you get my letter?' her father asked. 'I sent it on the 18th. There was money in an envelope for your mother. Never mind. My kitbag's full of good things. I've a leg of lamb, a cake, some chocolate and, of course your presents. So now let's get home and see what's happening.'

There could not have been a more joyful Christmas homecoming in any family, before or since. Their father could not get into the house for the children's hugs and kisses, tears, and shouts.

'Billy,' said father, 'I can't tell you how proud I am of you. I'll go and buy back those rabbits for you it if costs me twice what you paid for them. Now let's go and see how things are inside the house.'

Granny Sawyer was standing in the kitchen. Her grey hair was dishevelled, and the white apron over her long black dress was crumpled and stained. But tears of happiness flowed down her old lined face, and from upstairs came the cry of a baby.

'God be praised, Jack,' she cried. 'He's sent us the best Christmas present we could want. You're home and Sally's fine. She's had the baby—come upstairs and see. You can all come up. It's a dear little baby boy.'

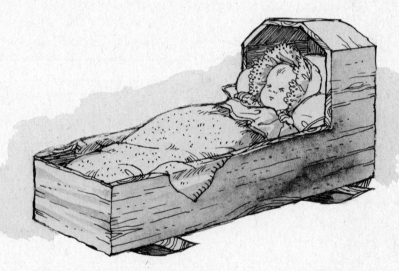

The Kissing Bush

Kissing beneath the mistletoe used to be a very important custom. A girl who was not kissed might never marry, and a young man who missed his chance to kiss a girl was thought to be in for an unlucky year. No girl ever refused a kiss:

> *It has been writ that any man*
> *May blameless kiss what maid he can,*
> *Nor anyone shall say him 'no'*
> *Beneath the holy mistletoe.*

About a hundred years ago, however, mistletoe became hard to get. In some parts of the country it hardly grew at all, and people living in towns had difficulty in getting into the countryside to find any.

Because of this, *kissing bushes* were made to replace the customary boughs of mistletoe. The kissing bush (or bough) was of various forms, but it was usually made of evergreens arranged on a frame of crossed hoops. Various items hung in the hoops, such as red apples, oranges, nuts, toys, and trinkets.

It was important to have a small sprig of mistletoe, if one could be bought or found. This would be hung from the centre of the bush.

Make this Traditional Kissing Bush

You will need:
Five pieces of pliable wire (cut in 122cm lengths)
red ribbon
seven apples
evergreens (the small leafed type, such as box, is best)
a sprig of mistletoe
strong tape
very fine wire (green garden wire is best)
wire cutters or pliers
a bodkin
a spool of thread.

To make the frame:
Bend the lengths of wire into a circle with an overlap of 5cm. Tape across the join. Check that all five circles are the same size.

Use one of the hoops as the central circle and take a second hoop, fitting it outside and at right angles to the first (Fig 1). Bind the points of intersection with fine wire and tape them so that they are held firmly in place.

Use a third hoop to complete the globe shape, as shown in Fig 2. Again make the intersections and bind with tape.

The fourth and fifth hoops go exactly half-way between the sections of your globe shape (Fig 3). Make sure the spaces between the hoops around the central horizontal circle are equal. Wire and tape the last intersections and the points where the hoops cross at top and bottom. Cover the globe-shaped frame with evergreens (box, holly, or ivy are best) until no wire can be seen.

Choose the smallest small apples you can find (a traditional number is seven) and hang the

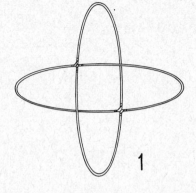

apples on red ribbon from the top, inside the globe. Thread the ribbon from the top of the apple through the core, and fasten it underneath with a knot. It you have a sprig of mistletoe, hang it from the bottom of the kissing bush.

Traditional kissing bushes were not highly decorated, but over the years they have been made to look more and more colourful.

You could, if you wish, add ribbons, tinsel, and glass Christmas tree decorations. If you have small tin candle clips, you could place candles around the spaces on the central horizontal hoop. But remember that small children should only light candles when adults are present. (You will find a colour photograph of the kissing bush on pp 34–5.)

Legends about the Christmas Tree

There are many stories and legends which tell why the fir tree was chosen as the tree of Christmas. In one such legend, Saint Boniface, in the eighth century, was travelling through northern Europe. He came across some Druids about to perform a sacrifice beneath their sacred tree, the oak. Boniface seized an axe and cut down the oak. In its place he planted a fir to symbolize the new Christian religion. Many of the legends of the Christmas tree concern the Christ Child.

The Christ Child and the Woodman

One cold Christmas Eve, long long ago, a woodman and his family were sitting round their blazing log fire when suddenly there was a knock on the door of their cottage. Wondering who on earth would be calling on them so late and in such snowy weather, the woodman went to see who it was.

Standing outside was a little child. He was shivering with cold, and he looked hungry and tired out. The astonished woodman led the child inside.

'Who can he be? Why is he alone in the forest?' exclaimed the woodman's wife.

At once she set her children to rubbing back life into the boy's poor frozen limbs, while she busied herself in making him some hot milk to drink.

'He can sleep in my bed tonight,' said the eldest son. 'I will sleep on the floor.' So the exhausted child was put into a warm bed and he fell asleep at once.

In the morning, the woodman's family was awakened by the sound of beautiful voices singing.

'It is like the sound of angels,' they whispered.

Suddenly the room was filled with light. When they looked at the child they had sheltered, they realized that it was the Christ Child himself.

The woodman and his family fell to their knees in awe, but the Christ Child went outside to a small fir tree and touched its branches. At once the tree shone with a great light.

'You took me into your home,' said the Christ Child. 'You gave me the gifts of food, shelter, warmth, and kindness. Now here is my gift to you—a tree that will remind you at Christmas time that you took me into your hearts. May it shine to show my love for you, and may it bear gifts as a token of your love for one another.'

The Legend of Tinsel

There once lived a woman whose husband had died. The poor woman was left to bring up a large family of children all by herself. She worked her fingers to the bone, and made sure that her children were always fed and well-clothed.

Although she was poor, the woman was determined that her children would have a happy time at Christmas. After the children had gone to bed, she worked late into the night to make them little presents.

Just before Christmas, she secretly prepared a Christmas tree and put it ready to surprise her family on Christmas Day. Unfortunately, spiders visited the tree. They crawled from branch to branch and spread their webs all over it.

The Christ Child saw the hidden tree. He knew the women would be upset to find it covered in spiders' webs, and so he turned the webs all to shining silver. On Christmas morning, when the woman came for the tree, she was overjoyed to find it looking more beautiful than she could ever have imagined.

The Fir Tree's Candles

On the night of the Holy Birth all living things, both plants and animals, went to the stable at Bethlehem to honour the Christ Child and take him gifts. Among the trees that crowded into the stable was the little fir tree. The palm tree gave dates to the baby. The olive tree gave its fruit. The cherry held out is beautiful blossom. But the fir tree had nothing to give. It was weary from its journey, and the larger trees pushed it aside.

At last an angel saw the fir tree weeping amber tears along its stem. He felt sorry for the tree, and asked the stars to come down and rest on its branches. The stars did so, and shone like candles. The fir tree stood, tall and straight, and held out its branches proudly for the stars to settle on.

The Baby Jesus saw the glowing tree and laughed with joy. Then he blessed the fir tree and declared that at Christmas, fir trees should always be lit to please the children.

The Christmas Reindeer Flying School.
(Beginners' class.)

Flying Teacher 'Chock's Away' teaching the first flying movements by O'Grady Method. (O'grady says, flap your front legs up and down..)

learner springs.

baby learner

This year's winner of the Father Christmas look alike contest.

Footprints in the Snow

What were the mysterious footprints in the snow that appeared overnight across the county of Devon? Whatever or whoever made them travelled over a hundred miles, crossed a two-mile estuary and even walked up the sides of houses. And why did people shudder when they saw the footprints, and close their doors in fear?

One of the strangest of all the unsolved mysteries in England occurred in Devon during the winter of 1854–5. During the night of 8 February, after a day of heavy frost and intense cold, there was a fall of snow. When people awoke the next morning they noticed, to their amazement, a trail of strange footprints. None of the townsfolk or villagers had ever seen footprints like them, for they appeared to have been made by a creature with hooves, walking upright on two legs.

Although the hooves followed a zig-zag path through the freshly fallen snow, they seemed to be going in a single direction as if making a journey across the countryside.

Indeed, as the morning wore on, it was discovered that whatever had made the prints had travelled over a hundred miles. Even more extraordinary was that the prints sometimes went straight across the roofs of houses or the tops of haystacks. When they came to high walls, hedges, or fences they simply continued on the other side.

The mysterious footprints were seen as far afield as Totnes in the South and Budleigh in the North. Whatever had made the marks had travelled over a hundred miles. Villagers near Kenton followed the trail to the edge of the Estuary of the River Exe where it is two miles wide. Here the prints ended. The baffled villagers later learned that the prints continued on the other side as if the creature had swum across!

In one place the trail vanished into thick bracken and under-growth. Dogs were sent to search the thicket, but they are said to have howled dismally and refused to go in. In another place a party of trackers discovered that the prints went *through* a haystack instead of over the top. Later they came across footprints that went across the roofs of barns and houses.

All kinds of theories about the footprints were put forward. One suggestion was that they were made by large birds such as swans or gulls. Other ideas were that animals, such as rabbits, foxes, hares, or even a donkey were the cause.

It was even suggested that the prints could be those of a kangaroo which had perhaps escaped from a travelling zoo!

People's fears were not lessened when one investigator said: 'No known animal could have traversed the extent of country in one night, besides having to cross an estuary two miles broad. Neither does any known animal walk in a line of single footsteps. . . . Birds could not have left these marks, as no bird's foot leaves the impression of a hoof . . .'

And when someone asked if a change in temperature could have caused the tracks of quite ordinary animals to melt slightly and change into extraordinary-looking hoof-prints, it was proved they hadn't. The prints of cats and dogs that had been out on the same night were absolutely normal.

At last the famous naturalist Sir Richard Owen, claimed that the prints were made by badgers. He pointed out that a badger places its hind feet in the marks made by its forefeet, and also that a badger makes a print larger than the actual size of its pad. The tracks, he asserted, were not made by one badger, but by several, and although they hibernate they sometimes venture out in search of food.

Was the expert right? The local people nodded their heads, but they went on wondering. After all, how could a prowling badger climb a wall, or a haystack, or up the side of a house? And if that *was* the answer, why had such footprints never been noticed before?

And, come to think of it, why have such footprints never been seen since?

Make this Snowman

Make this snowman (pictured on the opposite page) as a centre-piece for a Christmas party or a winter decoration. His head can be removed and his body filled with sweets or small party gifts. (You will find a colour photograph of him on pp 34–5.)

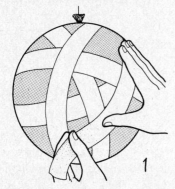

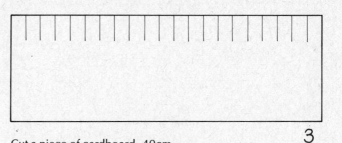

Begin by covering one large and one small balloon with strips of newspaper dipped in wallpaper paste (Fig 1). Use double layer strips about 5cm wide. Make sure you cover all the spaces as you work around the balloon. Cover each balloon with at least four layers of newspaper.

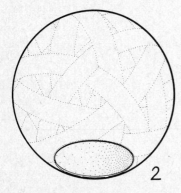

Let these balloon shapes dry overnight. Deflate both balloons. Cut a circle about 10cm wide where the neck of the smaller balloon came through the shell (Fig 2). Do the same to the larger body shape.

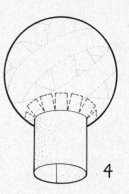

Cut a piece of cardboard, 40cm long and 13cm deep, along the top edge at 2cm intervals (Fig 3). Roll this strip into a tube and fit it snugly into the neck-hole of the smaller balloon. Mark the exact point of overlap. Take out and glue to form a cylinder.

Put glue on the outside flaps that you previously cut in the top. Slip them into the hole in the head and stick firmly to the inside of the shell (Fig 4). This forms a neck that will go inside the hole in the body and keep the head in place.

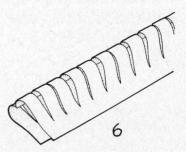

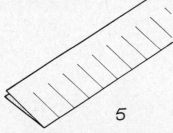

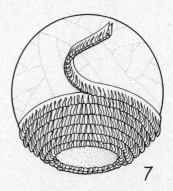

To cover the snowman, take used white tissue paper curls, made from 7cm strips of tissue folded in half lengthwise and cut ⅔ of the way across the strip along the folded edge at 1cm intervals (Fig 5). Fold several strips together and cut all at once to save time. Turn the strips wrong side out to make them fluff up (Fig 6). Glue these strips around both shapes, starting in each case at the neck holes and overlapping each round, until both shapes are covered (Fig 7).

Draw a line 2cm above the bottom edge. Cut from the bottom edge to this line at 2cm intervals (Fig 9). Form this strip into a tube, and glue. Make sure it has just the 2cm overlap you allowed. Fold down the flaps around the small circle. Slip them inside the hat tube, and glue in place to form the top of the hat (Fig 10). Fold out the bottom glue flaps and glue them so that the tube rests in the centre of the large circle, which then becomes the hat brim (Fig 11). The hat can now be glued to the snowman's head.

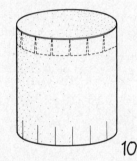

10

9

To dress the snowman, cut a long narrow strip of cloth to make a scarf. Glue on eyes, nose, mouth, and buttons. You can use black jelly drops, but old buttons or paper will do.

The top hat is made from black paper and thin cardboard. Cut a circle about as wide as the snowman's head out of cardboard and a second circle about 6cm smaller in diameter. Cover the large circle with black paper on both sides. Glue the small circle onto black paper. When you cut it out, leave an extra centimetre of black paper from the edge to the cardboard circle at 2cm intervals to form glue flaps (Fig 8). Cut a piece of black paper large enough to go around the small circle plus 2 extra cm overlap. This piece should be about 13cm high.

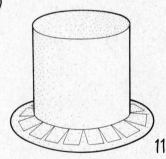

11

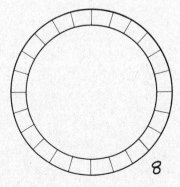

8

Note: Instead of paper curls you can use thin layers of cotton wool brushed over with wallpaper paste and moulded to cover the snowman shape. To give it extra sparkle, sprinkle with Epsom Salt crystals and put aside to dry overnight.

Ski-run

Can you find your way down the ski-run from the start (A) at the top left-hand corner, to the finish (A), at the bottom right-hand corner? As you can see, the first move is on to a white square, so your next move must be on to a

black square; next on to a white square, then on to a black square, and so on, alternately.

You may move upwards, downwards and sideways, but not diagonally. (And of course

you can only move one square at a time.) When you have mastered ski-run A, try going from start (B), at the top right-hand corner, to the finish (B), at the bottom left-hand corner.

Winter Morning

No one has ever been here before,
Never before!
Snow is stretching, pure and white,
From the back door
To where that elm-tree by the coppice-fence
Stands black and bare,
With never a footprint, never a clawprint
Anywhere!
Only the clean, white page of snow
In front of me,
With the long shadow of a single tree
For company.

At Nine of the Night I opened my Door

At nine of the night I opened my door
That stands midway between moor and moor,
And all around me, silver-bright,
I saw that the world had turned to white.

Thick was the snow on field and hedge
And vanished was the river-sedge,
Where winter skilfully had wound
A shining scarf without a sound.

And as I stood and gazed my fill
A stable-boy came down the hill.
With every step I saw him take
Flew at his heel a puff of flake.

His brow was whiter than the hoar,
A beard of freshest snow he wore,
And round about him, snow-flake starred,
A red horse-blanket from the yard.

In a red cloak I saw him go,
His back was bent, his step was slow,
And as he laboured through the cold
He seemed a hundred winters old.

I stood and watched the snowy head,
The whiskers white, the cloak of red.
'A Merry Christmas!' I heard him cry.
'The same to you, old friend,' said I.

The Very Proper Christmas

'Tripe and onions?' said Great-uncle Wilfred. 'You can't have tripe and onions for Christmas dinner!'

'We always do,' said Fiona. 'We all like it best.'

'And Ma makes a surprise pudding,' said Stewart. 'Last year it was ice-cream cake. It was lovely.'

'No Christmas pudding?' Great-uncle Wilfred went pale and sat down in the armchair. 'Bless my soul. You'll be telling me you don't have Christmas decorations next.'

'Well, we do—' said Fiona.

'And we don't,' said Stewart.

They looked at each other and grinned.

'We don't have paper chains and things,' Stewart explained. 'Just lots and lots of balloons filled with helium. They float in the living-room, up by the ceiling. It's *beautiful*.'

'And we paint murals all over the living-room walls,' Fiona butted in. 'One wall each. And after Christmas Daddy redecorates the room. I've got a marvellous idea for my wall this year.'

'Never heard such nonsense in my life,' said Great-uncle Wilfred faintly. 'What about paper chains? And stockings? And a tree?'

The children glanced uneasily at each other.

'Yes, we do have presents,' Stewart said carefully. 'Lots.'

Great-uncle Wilfred looked out suspiciously from under his bushy eyebrows. 'Go on,' he barked. 'What about the other things?'

'We have a Great Present Hunt,' Fiona said. 'We hide the presents we're giving and write *fiendishly* difficult clues. Riddles and poems and anagrams and all sorts. It takes us most of the day to solve them. So we don't really need stockings or a tree.'

Great-uncle Wilfred snorted. 'Never heard such rubbish in all me born days. Can't think what your parents are up to. All these years you've been missing a *proper* Christmas. I can see I'll have to speak to your mother.' He stomped off towards the kitchen.

'You don't think Ma will listen to him, do you?' Stewart said anxiously.

'Of course not . . . D'you think we should go and listen?'

'Fee! That's eavesdropping!' Stewart winked. 'Let's.'

They did not need to put their ears to the door. From half-way down the hall they could hear Great-uncle Wilfred thundering.

'. . . all my years in Patagonia . . . dreamed about *proper* English Christmasses . . . what do I find? . . . load of balderdash . . . what I say is, *What about the children?*'

Mrs McAllister said something softly and Great-uncle Wilfred spluttered. 'Don't *want* it? Never heard such piffle. All children like holly and stockings and Christmas pudding and—dash it all, the poor little things don't know what they're missing!'

Mrs McAllister came out of the kitchen and shut the door behind her. 'You've been listening!' she hissed.

'Ma, you won't take any notice of him, will you?'

'*Course* she won't,' said Fiona.

'Well, actually—' Their mother looked at them. 'I meant to talk to you about it anyway. Would you mind awfully if—?'

'Hysterically,' Stewart said.

'Dementedly,' said Fiona.

Their mother glanced over her shoulder. 'But *he* minds too. Dreadfully. And it's his first Christmas in England for forty years.'

The children shuffled their feet.

'He keeps saying he wants it for *us*,' Fiona muttered. 'So why can't we have what we like?'

'That's what people always say about Christmas.' Mrs McAllister smiled. 'They don't mean it. D'you think I'd let you paint the walls if I didn't enjoy it too? So what about letting Great-uncle Wilfred have his perfect Christmas? Just this once.'

The children looked at each other.

'Oh, all right,' Fiona said grumpily.

Great-uncle Wilfred did not need telling twice. He began to shop immediately, returning every day with armfuls of parcels. Once Mr McAllister said mildly, 'Do you think it's necessary to buy so *much* of everything, Wilfred?'

'Must do it properly.' Great-uncle Wilfred waved a huge hand. 'Don't worry, dear boy. Think what you'll save, not having to redecorate the living-room this year. I'm *economizing*.'

'Humph,' Mr McAllister said, and went back to his paper.

Great-uncle Wilfred turned to Fiona. 'Come on, then. And you, Stewart. It's time to stir the pudding.'

Fiona levered herself out of her chair and they followed him into the kitchen.

'Have a stir,' he chuckled, 'and you get a wish.'

Fionna looked down at the solid mixture which filled the washing-up bowl. 'We're going to eat *that* on Christmas Day?'

'Yes,' beamed Great-uncle Wilfred, 'and very delicious it will be.' He thrust the wooden spoon at her. 'Go on. Wish.'

Fiona dug the spoon into the stiff mixture. Stewart looked at her. 'What're you wishing, Fee?'

'I wished—' Fiona began, but Great-uncle Wilfred thrust a sticky hand over her face.

'Mustn't tell,' he said waggishly, 'or it won't come true.'

When the children came down to breakfast next morning, the kitchen was full of steam. Trails of condensation ran everywhere.

'Eugh!' said Fiona. 'What're you doing, Ma?'

Mrs McAllister sighed. 'Steaming the Christmas puddings.'

'Before breakfast?' Fiona stared.

'How long is it going on for?' Stewart said suspiciously.

'Eight hours, Great-uncle Wilfred says. At least.'

'That does it,' Fiona said. 'I'm off. Come on, Stew.'

They grabbed pieces of toast and set out to visit all the friends they could think of. When they came home, after a peaceful day, the house was ominously quiet.

'Ma!' shouted Fiona, 'We're back.'

There was no answer.

'Look,' Stewart said, 'a note.'

'*Gone out with Great-uncle Wilfred to buy more Christmas decorations.*'

'I don't feel very sure about this Christmas,' Fiona said slowly. 'D'you think Great-uncle Wilfred knows what he's doing?'

'It's all good, clean fun, my girl,' said Stewart. 'You don't know what you've been missing all these years, not having a kitchen full of

steam. Come on.' They went into the living-room.

Fiona flopped into a chair and bounced up, yelling. 'What—?'

'More traditional Christmas jollity.' Stewart chuckled. 'It's Great-uncle Wilfred's holly.'

Fiona muttered, scooping armfuls of holly off the chair. 'It's going to be a *disaster*. A catastrophe.' No sooner had she sat down again than the front door burst open.

'Sitting down?' Great-uncle Wilfred boomed. 'That won't do. We've got hundreds of decorations to put up.'

He began to tip garlands of coloured paper out of a carrier bag and Fiona looked at them crossly. 'Couldn't we do it tomorrow?'

'On Christmas Day?' Great-uncle Wilfred sounded shocked. 'Fiddlesticks. Run along and fetch the step-ladder, Stewart.'

They worked for an hour, pinning up loops of paper, swags of holly, bunches of mistletoe, until the whole ceiling was draped.

'There!' said Great-uncle Wilfred at last. 'Now that's what I call proper Christmas decorations.'

'Not bad,' Stewart said reluctantly. 'Fancy a cup of tea, Ma?'

'Lovely!' said Mrs McAllister. Great-uncle Wilfred goggled.

'Tea? There's no time for that. We've still got the Christmas tree to do. It's in the garden.'

He bounced off, and Mrs McAllister pulled a face at the children. 'Think you can stand it?'

'But it's what all children *love*.' Stewart said gravely.

There was a loud crash from the area of the front door. 'I say', came Great-uncle Wilfred's muffled voice, 'I seem to have got rather a *large* tree.'

'Eight foot tall,' Mrs McAllister whispered ruefully. 'I did tell him, but he wouldn't listen.' They went into the hall. Great-uncle Wilfred was completely invisible and the doorway was full of long branches, waving dangerously. 'Fetch the saw, Stew.'

After much hacking, they brought a rather bedraggled tree into the living-room. Great-uncle Wilfred looked proudly at it. 'I do like a big one. Now . . . the opposite end to the dining-table, I think. Get a box, Stewart. And some heavy stones.'

Wearily, Stewart and Fiona began to lug stones in from the back garden, while Great-uncle Wilfred urged them on with cheerful cries. 'That's it! Just a few more. Got to get it straight.'

First the tree lurched forwards. Then it lurched to the left. Finally, they managed to steady it.

'Nobody sneeze,' whispered Stewart.

'Baubles,' said Great-uncle Wilfred.

Fiona looked at him. 'I beg your pardon?'

'Got to hang it with baubles, girl. You know. Glass balls and tinsel and stuff. Got boxes and boxes of the things.'

'Whoopee,' said Fiona sarcastically.

By the time they had draped the Christmas tree with a glittering jumble of ornaments, it was half-past nine in the evening. Mr McAllister had come in earlier, taken one look at them and retreated to the kitchen. Now he called out, 'How about supper?'

'Yes please, Dad. I'm starving,' Stewart said.

'Piffle!' Great-uncle Wilfred roared. 'There's still the turkey to stuff. I've got my mother's recipe for rice and orange stuffing. Delicious! You can come and watch me.'

Propped uncomfortably in the kitchen, with plates in their hands, they watched Great-uncle Wilfred ladle rice into the turkey.

'Don't you think,' Mrs McAllister said gently, 'that you ought to *cook* the rice first?'

'Nonsense, girl.' Great-uncle Wilfred brushed her objections away. 'It'll cook while the turkey's roasting. Just need to put a bit of water in the tin, that's all.' He rammed in another handful of raw rice and orange peel, pushing hard to fit it in. 'Pass me the needle and thread.'

'Yes, but—' Mrs McAllister said. Then she stopped, shrugged and watched him stitching up the turkey.

Fiona gave a loud yawn. 'I'm going to bed.'

'Stockings.' Great-uncle Wilfred snapped the thread. 'Got to hang up your stockings. Brought my old football socks especially.'

He hurried the children upstairs to the room they shared when visitors came. With an air of triumph, he produced a huge pair of moth-eaten socks in alternate stripes of purple and mustard.

'How will Father Christmas know he has to call here?' Stewart said politely. 'He never has before.'

Great-uncle Wilfred winked and tied the socks to the footboard of the double bed. Then he tiptoed out and Fiona glared balefully at them. 'It's going to be a *terrible* Christmas. My wish, when I stirred the pudding, was no use at all. I wished—'

'Now, now,' Stewart said sleepily. 'Mustn't tell.'

Fiona woke up, quite suddenly, in the dark. There was someone in the bedroom, a tall, bearded shape, in strange, flowing garments. Terrified, she opened her mouth, but before she made a sound a hand clamped over her face.

'Ssh,' whispered Stewart in her ear. 'It's Father Christmas.'

'Who?' she whispered back.

'Great-uncle Wilfred, you idiot. Be quiet.'

With heavy, tiptoeing steps, the figure crashed into the footboard. 'Dash it!' came a loud mutter.

Stewart snored reassuringly and the figure began to move again. There were grunts and mutters as it pushed things into the socks. Fiona shoved a hand into her mouth to stop a giggle. With a final lurch, the figure dropped something heavy against the end of the bed. There was a loud pop. Then the feet shuffled away.

'Happy Christmas, Fee,' Steward yawned. 'See you in the morning.' He was asleep before she could reply.

When Fiona woke up again, Stewart was sitting on the end of the bed, unwrapping the things from his stocking. In one hand he held a popped balloon and in the other a bar of chocolate which he was munching determinedly.

'Chocolate before breakfast?' Fiona pulled a face. 'Yuck.'

'I'm going to need all the energy I can get today,' Stewart said solemnly. 'Just to keep up with Great-uncle Wilfred. Come on, Fee. Get unwrapping. He'll be very disappointed if you don't.'

Wearily, Fiona pulled herself out of bed and took the first parcel from the top of her stocking. She unwrapped it. It was a little plastic wrist-watch. She stared at it. Then, with a sigh, she took off her real watch, put it on the chest of drawers and buckled on the plastic one instead. 'It's going to be *awful*,' she said pathetically. '*Boring*. And after I wished—'

'Naughty, naughty!' Stewart wagged a finger at her. 'Mustn't tell. Great-uncle Wilfred'll catch you.'

They could hear him on the landing, marching up and down shouting, 'Everybody up! Got to put the turkey in before church.'

When they came back from church and opened the front door, the house was as hot as a furnace. Steam from the Christmas pudding steamer filled the air and the roaring of the oven sounded strangely loud. 'I'll just go into the kitchen,' Mrs McAllister said nervously.

'Let me,' chortled Great-uncle Wilfred. 'I'll go and take the turkey out of the oven.'

He strode into the kitchen doorway and then stopped dead. 'Oh,' they heard him say. 'Oh dear.' Everyone ran to look.

'You were certainly right about the rice cooking inside the turkey,' said Mr McAllister.

The rice had cooked perfectly. And, as rice does, it had swelled up. Swelled until it exploded the turkey and pushed open the oven door. There was a heap of rice and turkey on the floor, and the oven was jammed with the same mixture. From the back came a faint smell of scorching. 'Oh dear,' said Great-uncle Wilfred again.

Mrs McAllister walked briskly across the kitchen and turned off the oven. 'There'll be plenty left,' she said cheerily. 'If you all go and lay the table, I'll cook the sprouts and dish up.'

As she put the food on the table, Great-uncle Wilfred boomed, 'Can't start eating yet. Got to pull the crackers. Here.'

Holding out a red cracker for Stewart to clutch, he jerked his arm backwards and hit the gravy boat. It fell into Mr McAllister's lap, tipping a stream of hot gravy all over his knees.

'Sorry, my boy,' said Great-uncle Wilfred. 'You all right?'

'Fine,' said Mr McAllister, through clenched teeth. Great-uncle Wilfred beamed at him.

'All part of the fun and games. Have some turkey.' While Mr McAllister mopped surreptitiously at his knees, Great-uncle Wilfred ladled mounds of food on to everyone's plate. 'It's what I dreamed of, all those years abroad. A bit of English fun and games. A plateful of turkey. Crackers. Foreigners haven't got a *clue*. And never a bite of Christmas pudding anywhere abroad. Haven't tasted it for forty years. *Really* looking forward to that.'

'I'll never be able to fit in any pudding,' Fiona whispered to Stewart. 'Not after all this turkey.'

'Piffle, my girl. It's the best bit,' murmured Stewart. 'Great-uncle Wilfred's just dying to light that brandy.'

And he *was* keen. He whipped away their plates before they had quite finished and went to shut himself in the kitchen to prepare for the entry of the pudding. 'I only hope he's better with brandy than he is with gravy,' hissed Mr McAllister.

'Lights out!' bellowed Great-uncle Wilfred's voice. 'Here comes **the pudding!**'

He staggered into the darkened room, the Christmas pudding in one hand and, in the other, a saucepan full of blue flames.

'Wilfred,' Mrs McAllister said nervously, 'don't you think that's rather a *lot* of brandy?'

'Tommyrot, my girl,' boomed Great-uncle Wilfred. 'Got to have a good blaze. Here goes!'

He set the pudding down on the table and poured a smooth stream of pale fire on top of it. The flames ran down the sides like luminous, dancing water and swayed upwards in a great blue streak.

'Oh,' breathed Fiona, 'it's tremendous!'

'But there is a lot of brandy,' muttered Stewart.

There was. A lot. The flames roared high, catching the holly on top of the pudding and changing from blue to yellow. As Great-uncle Wilfred tipped on the last of the brandy, a column of fire shot upwards. It caught the festoon of paper chain which drooped over the table and set light to it. Before anyone had time to move, the flames ran the length of the room, shrivelling the paper chain to black flakes, and reached the Christmas tree. There was a sudden strong smell of hot pine.

'Ian!' said Mrs McAllister faintly.

Mr McAllister jumped up, opened the french windows and pushed the Christmas tree into the back garden. The next moment it went up in a great sheet of flame and the McAllisters stood watching.

The tree burned steadily. Strands of tinsel shrivelled and then became red hot, glowing through the yellow flames. As they dropped to pieces, the glass baubles started to shatter. With high, musical pinging noises they exploded, spraying fragments of shining coloured glass into the air: red, blue, silver and gold in a steady shower.

Then it started to snow, white flakes floating down as the glittering coloured glass shot up. Where glass met snowflake, there was a soft hissing, audible over the steady crackle of the flames.

'Amazing!' murmured Stewart.

'Fabulous!' whispered Fiona.

'Terrible!' moaned Great-uncle Wilfred. He was still at the table, his face wretched. 'I've ruined your Christmas. I'm a silly old man.'

Fiona stared. 'What are you talking about? It's *marvellous*. You've made my Christmas pudding wish come true.'

'I have?' He blinked at her. 'What was it?'

Fiona looked sheepish. '*I wish we could have some flaming excitement this Christmas!* But I never imagined an exploding Christmas tree bonfire. It's beautiful. Got any more ideas like that?'

Slowly, Great-uncle Wilfred smiled. 'In Patagonia,' he murmured, we had a torchlight procession at midnight on Christmas Eve. In fancy dress. . . .'

Fiona marched across the room and seated herself firmly on his lap. 'Tell me all about it!' she ordered.

The Yule Log

People often associate a blazing log fire with their idea of an old-fashioned Christmas. The Yule-log ceremony is rarely, if ever, observed today and yet the log is still a well-loved symbol of Christmas cheer, even if a real log on the hearth has now been replaced by a chocolate one on the table!

A great deal of tradition once surrounded the ceremony of bringing in the Yule-log. The log itself was chosen on Candlemas Day (6 February) of the same year, and it was put on a fire and made to burn until sunset. Then it was put out and stored away in readiness for Christmas.

> Kindle the Christmas brand, and then
> 'Till sunset let it burn
> Which quenched, then lay it up again.
> 'Till Christmas next return.

On Christmas Eve, the log would be brought inside. At first only a few willing hands would try to pull it along, and they would pretend that the log was 'stuck in the mire'. This would lead to a game called 'bringing in the carthorse'. More and more people would join in and, with a great deal of laughter and pretended heaving and straining, the log would slowly be dragged along.

Sometimes each member of the family would sit on the log in turn and sing a Yule song as the great log was pulled forward.

To bring good luck to the house, it was important that a fragment of wood from the old log of the year before was kept by. This was then used to light the fire on which the new log was to burn.

> Part must be kept, wherewith to tend
> The Christmas log next year;
> And if 'tis safely kept, the fiend
> Can do no mischief here!

Once the log was ablaze, songs would be sung, and everyone would be given hot spiced ale to drink to a Merry Christmas and a Happy New Year. In some places Yule cakes were eaten. These were little biscuits baked in the shape of the Baby Jesus.

The Yule-log ceremony indicated the beginnings of the fun and festivities, and the log would be kept burning throughout the entire twelve days of Christmas. Often the ceremony was followed by the company telling each other ghost stories and spine-chilling tales round the fire.

A Mexican Piñata

Each evening from 16 December until Christmas Eve, families in Mexico practise a custom called *las posadas*. The word *posadas* means *resting place* or *lodging*. The custom re-enacts the trials and hardships experienced by Joseph and Mary when they tried to find shelter and a lodging-place in Bethlehem.

Families visit each other's homes, calling at a different home each night. They carry lighted candles and, as they knock at the door, they call out to be let in. At first the host refuses to admit the callers, but finally they are allowed to enter.

Then all kneel before the *nacimiento* (the crèche) and they sing carols.

There are several variations of the *posadas* custom. Some involve an elaborate procession, others are simply homely occasions among friends and neighbours.

After the religious part of the *posadas* has ended, a celebration is held. During the festivities the children are allowed to play with the *piñata*. This is a colourfully decorated container filled with sweets and toys. The children are blindfolded and the *piñata* is hung up. One by one the children are allowed to try to break open the *piñata* with a stick. At last it is broken open, and its contents spill out so that the children can scramble for a prize.

Why not try this enjoyable Mexican custom at a party or Christmas celebration?

To make a *piñata* you will need:
wallpaper paste
newspaper
two balloons
card or coloured paper
tissue paper
string and sticky tape.

To get the basic shape for your *piñata* you will need to cover two balloons, one large and one small, with papier mâché. Mix wallpaper paste and dip strips of newspaper (about 5cms wide) into it. Wrap double-layer strips around the balloon, covering all spaces. If you hang the balloon from the ceiling with string, it will be easier to handle (Fig 1).

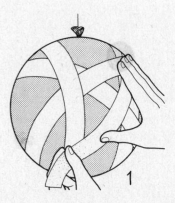

If you are filling your *piñata* with sweets or small gifts, it will need to be strong, so put at least four layers of newspaper on your balloons. When the shapes are completely dry, deflate and remove the balloons.

Here are three ideas for *piñatas* (Figs 2). You can use cardboard tubes for legs and necks. Tape all the parts together and bind them on with more paste-soaked strips. Cut a small hole in the back of the *piñata* so that you can fill it with sweets or small unbreakable presents.

2

If you want to make a typical Mexican *piñata*, it should be covered with paper curls. To do this fold 8cm strips of coloured tissue-paper lengthwise. Cut two-thirds of the way across the strip along the folded edge every centimetre, as shown in Fig 3. Fold several strips together and cut all at once to save time. Then turn the strips wrong side out to make them fluff up (Fig 4).

3

4

2

Glue these strips round the *piñata*, overlapping each round (Fig 5).

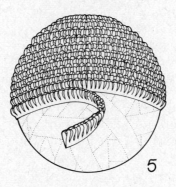

5

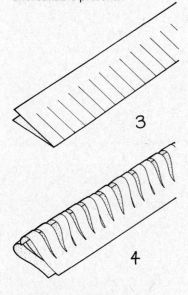

2

To finish off the *piñata*, use your imagination. Make beaks and eyes with foil, card, crêpe paper, or anything that is colourful. (For a colour photograph of a piñata, see pp 34–5.)

Fill with sweets and gifts, but remember, if you are going to play the game, be sure to fix the *piñata* firmly to the ceiling!

A Christmas Letter from Finland

Dear Marie,

Don't you think it's going to be a lot of fun when it's Christmas again? We have to buy a Christmas tree tomorrow because we always take it inside in the evening before 24th of December. It's exciting to decorate the tree. We do it with a lot of golden nuts, apples, angels, paper baskets and tinsel, and candles of course. Then we put a star on the top and 'tomtar' under the tree.

Do you know about the 'tomtar'? Well, a tomte is a very friendly kind of gnome who helps Father Christmas by telling him how the children have behaved during the year. When my mother wants my little brother to behave she just says that she happened to see a tomte outside the window: my brother stops being naughty!

In the windows of our house we put candles and stars made of straw. When we wake up on the morning of Christmas Eve, it's so beautiful to see the lighted tree against the darkness outside.

For Christmas lunch we have rice porridge with cinnamon and ground almond on top. In the porridge there should be one almond and the one who gets it will be married during the next year. But my mother always hides several almonds to stop us from quarrelling!

Later we all get dressed up, and then we collect all the Christmas gifts and put them under the tree. When it gets dark we light candles, and if there's any snow we make a lantern of snowballs on the porch.

Then we finally get our Christmas dinner. It's delicious! We have turkey or ham, potatoes, swede casserole and other things. The grown-ups eat salty herrings and caviar, but I don't like that.

After dinner we can finally open our gifts. It takes many hours because we do it by turns. It's fun to see what others get and watch their expressions. When all the gifts are opened we have gingerbread biscuits and Christmas tarts. On Christmas Eve we are allowed to stay up as late as we wish. How about you?

On New Year's Eve there's some extra fun. We stay awake until midnight and watch the New Year being celebrated with fireworks, and after that we cast our fortunes for the New Year. We melt tin, and pour it rapidly into a bucket filled with cold water. Then we just pick up a stiffened lump and try to guess what it represents. And of course we have to make New Year's promises. This year I promise to do my piano exercises. Are you going to make a New Year's promise?

It's always sad when Christmas is over. But there is an old saying, 'Hilarymas Day throws the Christmas away', and we throw out the tree and take down the decorations. And it's such a long time until next Christmas!

My love to your mother and Heidi for a Happy Christmas.

Gott Jul och Gott Nytt År,

Nadia

A Christmas Letter from France

Dear Nadia,

Thank you for your letter. Since the fifteenth of December we have been getting the crèche ready to set up. Now we are putting in the little figures of Joseph and Mary, the shepherds and Wise Men, and the donkey and cow. We don't add the Baby Jesus until midnight of Christmas Eve.

We've decorated our house with fairy lights, paper decorations, and candles. On the Christmas Tree we have put lots of beautiful gold and silver decorations, sugar walking-sticks, coloured balls, Père Noël on his sleigh, angels' hair, elves, crackers, little presents and candles— and on top a lovely big shining star!

It's very exciting on Christmas Eve wondering what Père Noël will bring us (providing we've been good!). We put the presents we are giving under the tree. Then we help to lay the table. We decorate it with candles and holly, and we put little surprise presents in everyone's place.

After this we sing carols and play games until it is time to go to midnight Mass. When we come home we sit down to a late supper which we call *le réveillon* (midnight party). We have roast turkey and chestnut stuffing, boudin blanc (white sausage), little chocolate cakes, wine, and, of course, a yule log cake.

We got to bed very tired. But first we put our shoes (well actually we put wellington boots) by the fire, and our stockings on our beds for Père Noël to fill with presents.

That is how we spend Christmas in France.

Joyeux Noël et Bonne Année!

Marie

Puddings and Pies

The Christmas puddings that we eat nowadays usually come in the shape of the basin in which they are cooked, but when you see pictures of traditional Christmas puddings they look like large footballs. This is because the pudding mixture was always tied up in a cloth or a bag and then boiled in a large pan (often in the tub that boiled the clothes on wash day). As the pudding cooked it would swell out to become nice and round in shape.

Christmas pudding used to be called 'plum pudding' because one of the main ingredients was dried plums or prunes. The name 'plum pudding' continued to be used even when people used raisins, currants, and sultanas instead of prunes.

Early puddings were nothing like the ones we enjoy today. They were long and round, and shaped like a thick sausage. They consisted of chopped-up meat, suet, oatmeal and spices, and they were cooked in the scalded intestines of a sheep or pig. These puddings were served hot at the beginning of a meal as the first course. If an unexpected visitor arrived when the pudding was on the table, he was usually invited to join the meal.

Puddings rather like the ones we eat at Christmas began to appear in the sixteenth century. Since they were boiled in a bag, they were known as 'bag puddings'. There is a legend about how such puddings came into being.

One Christmas Eve an English king found himself deep in a forest with only a little food for his journey. He knocked on the door of a woodman's cottage and asked for food and shelter. The woodman had few provisions, so the king's servant mixed together all that the woodman could spare with the little that the king had left. The result was a sticky mixture of chopped suet, flour, eggs, apples, dried plums, ale, sugar and brandy. This mixture was boiled in a cloth, and a delicious pudding was invented.

Putting silver charms into a pudding for good luck is a fairly recent custom. In the old days, items were mixed into Twelfth-night cake, and it was part of the fun to see who had what in each slice of cake:

a bean for the king
a pea for the queen
a clove for the knave
a twig for the fool
a rag for the slut.

Christmas puddings always used to be made on the Sunday nearest to St Andrew's Day. It was called 'Stir-Up Sunday' because in the prayer book for that day it says, 'Stir up, we beseech Thee, O Lord, the will of thy faithful people.' Every member of the family would be sure to stir the mixture and make a secret wish.

Here is the recipe for King George the First's Christmas pudding, in 1714:

- 1 lb of eggs
- 1½ lb shredded suet
- 1 lb dried plums
- 1 lb raisins
- 1 lb mixed peel
- 1 lb currants
- 1 lb sultanas
- 1 lb flour
- 1 lb sugar
- 1 lb breadcrumbs
- 1 teaspoon mixed spice
- ½ a grated nutmeg
- ½ pint milk
- ½ teaspoon of salt
- the juice of a lemon
- a large glass of brandy

Let the mixture stand for 12 hours. Then boil for 8 hours and boil again on Christmas Day for 2 hours. The mixture will yield 9 pounds of pudding.

Here are some of the 'permitted ingredients' printed on the foil wrapping of a Christmas pudding bought in a supermarket: dried egg, soya flour, hydrolized milk, mixed dried fruit, caramel colouring, monosodium glutamate, flavouring, added preservatives.

Mince pies are descended from Christmas pies, which contained a variety of meats as well as fruit and spices. Christmas pies were very much bigger than the tiny mince pies we eat today. One pie is recorded as having among its ingredients: a hare, a pheasant, a capon, two rabbits, two pigeons, two partridges, the livers of all these animals, as well as eggs, pickled mushrooms, and spices. Sometimes these pies could weigh as much as a hundred kilogrammes. They needed iron bands to hold them together while they were baking.

Little Jack Horner

Little Jack Horner
Sat in a corner,
Eating of Christmas pie:
He put in his thumb,
And pulled out a plum,
And said,"What a good boy am I!"

Jack Horner was steward to the Abbot of Glastonbury, and he had to take a pie to King Henry VII as a present from the Abbot. Under the crust were the title deeds of twelve manors sent to the King in the hope that he would not pull down Glastonbury Abbey. It is said that King Henry received only eleven deeds. What happened to the missing deed? Could that be why Jack Horner was so pleased with himself?

Christmas pies used to be oblong or square in shape. They came to be called 'crib pies' because they were similar in shape to the manger. Crib pies were disapproved of by the Puritan Parliament, especially those which had a little pastry figure to represent the Babe placed in the hollow on top.

After 1660, Christmas pies came to be called *minced pies*. They contained ingredients similar to the ones we use today. Here is an old recipe: a pound of beef suet chopped fine, a pound of raisins, a pound of currants, a pound of apples chopped fine to taste, two or three eggs, 'all-spice' ground very fine, salt, sugar to taste, and as much brandy as you like.

As time went on, mince pies became smaller and smaller. Another name for them was 'wayfarers' pies' since they were given to visitors during the Christmas holiday. It was thought to be lucky to eat twelve mince pies in twelve different houses during the twelve days of Christmas to ensure a happy twelve months for the year ahead.

Christmas in Prison

Far from home in a Chilean prison, I looked forward to Christmas in a way that I had not done since I was a child, lying in bed and dreaming of Christmas trees and carols, of parcels and tinsel, and most of all a roast turkey and Christmas pudding. I could imagine so well my family doing last minute Christmas shopping and the happy chaos of children wrapping carefully chosen gifts and running inquisitive fingers over mysterious packages. Every time the wardress entered the compound, I thought they had come for me and that I would be whisked away and put on a plane for England.

So it was that when on 23 December I heard on the lunchtime news that I was to face further charges, the nature of which had not been disclosed, I broke down and wept.

In a little while I pulled myself together and tried to put on a brave face. I knew perfectly well that I was being extremely childish and selfish. I knew now that it was only a matter of time before I gained my liberty, whereas for my fellow prisoners it would be many months or even years. The possibility that some of them might even be killed because of their political activity was too terrible to think about.

The atmosphere in the camp was unusually tense. Word had come through that there was going to be a Christmas amnesty. Everyone was trying to remain calm, while hoping against hope that their names might be on the list. All day we had been wondering who would be released. Those who had been held for over a year sat discussing whether the fact that they had been held so long made it almost certain that they would be released or if, conversely, it meant that they were considered dangerous and would be held even longer.

Suddenly, at about six o'clock there was a cry. 'The List! The List!' and we ran to where a group of girls were crowded round a small transistor radio. The reading had already begun. They were reading the names of the men as well, and we listened intently, for many of the girls had husbands or brothers in the men's section of the prison. Every so often there would be a scream of delight, followed by cries of exasperation, as some lucky person gave voice to her delight, and so drowned the name of the next person on the list. I was sitting

on the ground next to my friend Marcia when her name was read. She was not expecting to be released and when she heard her name there was a breathless gasp of joy and disbelief.

When the list ended, pandemonium broke loose. There were thirty girls on the list and they rushed frantically to organize their things, for it was the custom to release people without warning so that they could not smuggle messages out. Precious pieces of embroidery or crochet were hurriedly packed, and friends sped across the courtyard with tiny mementoes made of leather or wool or whatever was at hand. All spare clothing was hastily given away, for it was an unwritten law that anything that could be spared was left behind. Many of the prisoners were very poor and those who arrived from the torture centres had only the clothes in which they had been arrested, and after several weeks worn both day and night these were usually in a sad state.

It was not long before the door of the compound opened and the camp commander appeared. We were called on parade and then he read out the list of those who were to go. They were sent to fetch their things, and while we stood to attention they were escorted away to the main offices. There were no final hugs or goodbyes. The girls had learnt that such 'disorderly' behaviour resulted in suspension of visits from relatives, or a day in the calabozo, the underground cell which was used for punishment.

When the excitement of the departure was over, we resettled ourselves. It was a relief in many respects. We had been 120 women in a camp built to hold 80, so the departure of the 30 meant that there would be a bed for everyone and an end to sleeping on the floor. The dramas of the day were not over, however. The door opened again and Georgina came in, carrying her new baby daughter. She had gone into labour two nights previously and had been taken off to hospital. Now that her baby was born she returned to prison to share a room with five other girls. The joy of the girls knew no bounds. Susanna, who was a midwife, proudly took the tiny Javiera in her arms and displayed her to the assembled group.

At last things were quiet, and we busied ourselves wrapping up our presents. It had been decided that each girl should make one present and that these would be collected and redistributed during the party on Christmas Eve. That way everyone would receive a present. I had made leather pendants from scraps left over from the sandal 'workshop' and I gave one of these. When I had finished making a variety of pendants and key rings for my friends whom I hoped to see on Boxing Day, I looked around the bare compound and wished I had something to give it a festive air. Materials, however, were always in short supply as we had all of us become expert in making gifts or ornaments from scraps of wood, cloth, wire, or bone.

Being separated from the traditional English Christmas and from all forms of religious support, for no priests or ministers were allowed to hold services in the camp, I longed especially to make some Christian sign to mark the coming feast. I considered making a crib but again there was the problem of lack of materials, so I decided upon a poster. I borrowed a Christmas card from one of my friends and set about copying the design. Carefully I copied the card, and on a large piece of shelf paper drew the figure of the Christ Child holding on his lap a large, fat dove, the symbol of the peace for which we all longed. There was no paint to colour it, but I had a felt pen and shaded in a blue background. The pen was nearly dry but I refilled it with cologne. It still painted, though a little paler. The result was a rather pleasing mottled effect, and I fixed it to the wall with some stolen pins.

Christmas Eve dawned and as soon as breakfast was cleared away the girls began to prepare for the party. For weeks they had hoarded cans of *manjar*, the delicious spread which the Chileans make by boiling cans of condensed milk for hours, and other goodies. Now they gathered their resources together to make a pudding for 80 people. I watched, fascinated. They took two tin trays and covered them with broken biscuit; then came a couple of cans of peaches and the *manjar*. My thoughts went guiltily to the two Harrods tinned Christmas cakes which the British ambassador had given me and which I had not put in to the common pool because it seemed such a waste. I stood there and battled with my conscience, and eventually honour (and the knowledge that no one would join me in a secret feast) triumphed and I brought them along and presented them to the cake-makers. I could not resist making it very clear that these were very expensive, very special English cakes, the like of which was not made in Chile. They knew I found it difficult to be an anonymous member of the community and thanked me suitably. We were not allowed alcohol, so the very smell of brandy from the opened tins made us giggly, and I stood by while the rich dark product of some secret Harrods recipe was stirred sacrilegiously in with the biscuits and condensed milk.

As I stood watching the final touches being made to the pudding, I was called by the wardress and told that the camp commander had graciously allowed the army chaplain to celebrate mass. As I was the most vocal of the Christians (I had frequently done battle with the colonel to try to persuade the imprisoned priests to say mass for us) I was told to prepare.

Delighted, I gathered a band of helpers and we carried a table out into the exercise yard. Someone had a clean sheet and we arranged a Christmas altar bedecked with branches pulled from bushes in the prison yard. I pinned my poster on to the front and laid out the crucifix with the Christ made in copper wire that I had made the day I arrived at the camp. Determined that the service should both give glory to God and comfort to the prisoners, I conferred with Beatriz, who had been allowed to have her guitar for Christmas. We made a list of hymns that most people knew, and the 'choir' went into one of the rooms to practise.

At about twelve the priest came, and we sat on benches and on the ground in what shade we could find, for the sun was very hot, and joined with the priest in prayers of the mass. Seldom have I participated in a more moving act of worship, for we were joined, Christians and Marxists, believers and atheists, in praise and thanksgiving and desperate asking to our God or whatever force drives the universe. There were many tears as we sang familiar hymns and especially the 'Song of Joy' which has become like a protest song in Chile, for it speaks of the day when all men will again be brothers. At the communion Georgina carried her baby to the altar with her, and I think there was no one who did not see in Javiera the defenceless babe of Bethlehem.

In the afternoon we prepared the compound, arranging the tables in one corner for the food and the benches around the walls. The prison kitchen made no gesture for the festive season, but no one bothered to eat the tasteless soup because we knew that there were trays and trays of open sardine sandwiches and delicious biscuits with cheese or hard-boiled egg. Everyone dressed with care, for the lack of menfolk was no excuse for depression, and at eight o'clock the compound was full of elegant ladies happily drinking fruit juice and talking to their friends.

At nine o'clock the 'pudding' was produced, and it was as though the miracle of the loaves and the fishes had been repeated, for the ambassador's two small cakes fed the eighty of us with some to spare. After supper Beatriz played her guitar, and we all sang with a rare joy, for even singing had been prohibited for months in an effort to lower morale.

Then at exactly ten o'clock came the most moving ceremony I have ever witnessed. It was the hour which had been set to sing for the benefit of the men, so near and yet so far, in their compound a hundred yards away. Standing on tables and benches so that their voices would carry further, the girls sang as if their lungs would burst and their hearts would break. Their song filled the night air and rose towards the star-filled sky as they sent their Christmas message of love and hope to their menfolk and to those who had no one to love them behind the high concrete wall. On and on they sang, finishing with the mighty chorus of the song written in prison: 'Animo, Negro José—Take heart, Joe my love'.

Suddenly the order was given to be silent and we waited with breath held. I found the tears rolling down my cheeks as, faintly on the wind, I heard the answering song of the men.

After the singing we danced. I was wearing a dreadful T-shirt with a black-habited nun riding a motor bicycle and the legend 'Nun Power' emblazoned across my bosom, and I rocked and rolled as I had not done for twenty years. (The shirt was a gift from an American friend and it so pleased my fellow prisoners that I was made to wear it.)

As I flung myself in gay abandon round the compound the girls drew to the side and clapped, for my dancing was so enthusiastic and funny that it had become a cabaret turn. Delighted to be a source of entertainment I gyrated until I was so dizzy that I could no longer stand and collapsed in a breathless heap on the ground.

Then, at five minutes to eleven, we fled like Cinderellas to our bunks and as I lay exhausted in the darkness, looking at the familiar glow of the last illicit cigarette in the opposite bunk, I knew that this would be the Christmas that I would remember with the greatest nostalgia of my life.

Dr Sheila Cassidy returned to England on 30 December 1975 after her imprisonment by the Chilean Military Government.

African Christmas

Here are no signs of festival,
No holly and no mistletoe,
No robin and no crackling fire,
And no soft, feathery fall of snow.

In England one could read the words
Telling how shepherds in the fold
Followed the star and reached the barn
Which kept the Saviour from the cold,

And picture in one's mind the scene—
The tipsy, cheerful foreign troops,
The kindly villagers who stood
About the Child in awkward groups.

But in this blazing Christmas heat
The ox, the ass, the bed of hay
The shepherds and the Holy Child
Are stilted figures in a play.

Exiles, we see that we, like slaves
To symbol and to memory,
Have worshipped, not the incarnate Christ,
But tinsel on the Christmas tree.

Nine Men's Morris

Nine men's morris is one of the oldest board games in Europe. Why not make yourself a board and enjoy the skill and strategy of this old and enjoyable game?

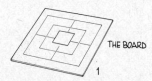

THE BOARD

1

To make your board
Use a square piece of cardboard. (You may like to use hardboard or wood.) Use felt pen or coloured sticky tape and mark out three squares, one inside the other. Connect the centres of all four sides of the squares with straight lines.

The 'men' or pieces
Either use draughts pieces, or make counters by cutting 1.5cm lengths of thick dowel. You will need nine black and nine white pieces.

The object of the game is to capture all but two of your opponent's men, or manoeuvre so that it becomes impossible for your opponent to move any of his pieces.

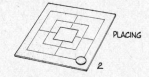

PLACING

2

TO PLAY

Placing. Play begins by 'placing' the men on the board. Players decide which one of them is to start. That player begins by placing ONE of his own men on any intersection on the board. The second player then places his piece on an intersection.

Each player then takes it in turn to place one man of his own colour on the board at an intersection not already occupied.

The AIM of each player is to get THREE of his men into a straight line along one of the lines of the board, and so form a 'mill'.

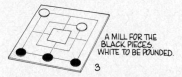

A MILL FOR THE BLACK PIECES. WHITE TO BE POUNDED.

3

Pounding Once a player has formed a mill, he may then 'pound' his opponent by taking an enemy piece from the board. A player may not pound (remove) an opponent's man that is part of a mill (unless there is no other piece available). A piece that has been pounded is dead and may not be used again during the game. Players continue until all the men have been placed on the board (except any that have been pounded during placing).

Moving Players may now move alternately. The object is to form new mills and so pound opponent's pieces.

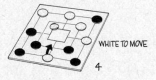

WHITE TO MOVE

4

A move is made from the existing position on the board to any adjoining intersection that is vacant. Players may create new mills by breaking an existing mill.

Play ends when one player is left with only two men on the board, or until one player's pieces are so blocked by his opponent's men that he can make no further moves.

Should a player's only remaining pieces form a mill and it is his turn to move, he must do so, even though he has to lose his piece and concede the game on his opponent's next move.

Hopping At the point where a player has ONLY THREE MEN LEFT, he may, if his opponent agrees, employ 'hopping'. This means that the losing player is no longer restricted to moving his men along a line to an adjacent point of intersection, but may now 'hop' to any vacant spot on the board. The ability to move anywhere gives this player an advantage and so restores his chance of winning.

End of play A player loses when he is reduced to having only two pieces or is so blocked in that he can make no further moves. (If hopping has been allowed the game ends when one player has only two pieces left on the board.)

Ghostly Tales round the Fireside

The Yule log has been brought inside and is blazing on the fire. The supper has been cleared away, and the noise and laughter are gone. Outside, the night is clear, still, and very cold. Inside, the clocks can be heard, and the flames leaping upwards cast dancing shadows on the ceiling. What better time to settle down in the glow of the fire and listen to a ghostly story or spine-chilling tale before going to bed?

Christmas Eve is the traditional time for telling ghost stories because it is said that no ghost or spirit walks abroad on that night. That is what they say. And perhaps it is true. But on a dark night like this, who can tell?

The Master's Gift

Peter leaned against the massive wrought-iron gate and pushed it almost closed. He took good care that the latch did not engage so that he could, if he had to, run back down the drive and escape without hindrance. He thrust his cold hands deep into his trouser pockets and started up the long curved drive, his feet crunching in the crisp white snow.

There was still time to run!

He walked on, gradually drawing closer to the huge mansion which lay at the top of the drive. From time to time he glanced down over the hill to the village below. No one would see him from down there, would they? He hadn't thought of that! Thick snow had fallen overnight, draining the colours from the countryside; dissolving shapes of trees and buildings so that even the cottages looked prematurely aged with thatch of white and silver. Yet even in this stark weather, the team of men still toiled over the thin trench which sliced through the village street. His father had told him that soon a gas pipe would be laid in the trench, and then every household in the area would be lit by modern gaslight.

The boy now stood before the thick door of the mansion, his hand reaching up slowly for the iron ring which passed through the nose of the lion-head door knocker. He gripped the ring in his hand, hesitated awhile, then allowed it to drop. It crashed against the door-stud, and the sound echoed through the hallway.

Listening for the approach of footsteps, Peter tried to avoid gazing at the frozen snarl on the face of the lion door-knocker. When he had first thought of it, his plan had seemed so simple, so perfect. Now he was not so sure. He wished he had never thought of the idea.

There was no reply.

He smiled. A mixture of relief and yet disappointment flooded through him at the same moment. His mind was now made up. He would never pluck up courage to raise that iron ring again. Perhaps it was just as well there was no one at home; the old man was probably away for Christmas.

He turned away, ready to make the long journey back to the village. Then he stopped. From the corner of his eye he noticed that

the door was soundlessly opening.

Evidently the impact of his knocking had caused the door to open. It could not have been securely locked. Cautiously he approached the door, reaching out his hand to pull it shut. All he really wanted to do was to respond to the inner urge to run away. Yet he did not want to leave the door open, especially if there was no one at home.

As he pulled the door he caught a fleeting glance of his own reflection in the tall hallway mirror. He paused, admiring the effect. There was no doubt about it—his disguise was excellent. He looked every inch a beggar boy: the torn shirt and ill-fitting clothes lent him the appearance of forlorn hopelessness.

'Who's there?' A voice came out of nowhere. Peter stammered 'The . . . the door—it was open . . . I . . . It opened by itself.'

'It opened by itself, did it?' came the voice, accusingly. It sounded so close to him that Peter cried out in surprise. And yet where had it come from?

Then, as if from nowhere, an old man, bowed with age, carrying his years upon his shoulders like a heavy load, stood beside him. He seemed to have come from nowhere out of the rapidly failing light of the winter afternoon.

'Go inside, boy,' the old man said, impatiently gesturing toward the open door.

Reluctantly Peter stepped into the dark hall. The fading light from the open door showed the magnificently carved wooden panels which lined the walls from floor to ceiling.

'Why have you come here?' the old man mumbled, shuffling past Peter and motioning him to follow. 'What do you want from me?'

'I came to sing carols,' Peter told him.

'Carols?' the old man paused before a door and signalled Peter to go in. 'Is it Christmas again? So soon?'

It was hot in the kitchen. Flames eagerly licked at the logs in the range, and a kettle boiled and bubbled, its lid clattering.

'Why come all the way up here to sing carols?' the old man asked. He pointed to a chair, waited until Peter was seated, then went to the fire and stabbed the poker into the white-hot logs, making them spit and crackle.

'I'm singing for my mother,' Peter said quickly.

'Your mother? Is she here?'

Peter shook his head.

'Then why come here to sing for her? She can't hear you from here, I'm sure of that. Unless you sing very loudly, of course?'

'She doesn't have to hear me,' said Peter.

Defeated by such logic, the old man scratched his head, his gnarled, bony fingers tousling the thin strands of snow-white hair. 'What nonsense is this?' he asked. 'You come all the way up to my house to sing carols for your mother, yet she cannot hear you?'

'I sing to earn money for her,' Peter explained. Inwardly he sighed. Would he ever make the old man understand? Digging his fingernails into the palms of his hands to prevent himself blushing, he prepared now to tell his lies. He hated lying, yet this was the only way. He had to do it.

'My mother is very ill,' he said. 'If she doesn't get medical help soon, she will lose her sight. I am singing to earn enough money to pay for the operation.'

'And it is expensive—this operation?' The old man held out a steaming bowl of soup. 'Come, drink this. You look frozen to the marrow, boy.'

'Yes, it is very expensive,' Peter replied. He was blushing furiously now, yet determined to continue with his plan.

'So now you wander through the snow, singing your dear little heart out, collecting pennies to save the sight of your mother?'

'That's right,' Peter said between mouthfuls of soup. It was good soup, strongly flavoured with onions and spices. Glancing up, he noticed that the old man's back was turned to him and that those frail old shoulders were shaking. He felt ashamed that he was the cause of the old man's sadness and reached into his pocket to offer his handkerchief to him. 'Here,' he said. 'Take this.'

'Thank you, boy,' the old man said, wiping away the thin, salty tears, dabbing at his red-rimmed eyes. He held up the handkerchief, examining it afresh in the fading light of the window. 'So clean,' he said, almost to himself. 'So clean and white, like the snow. When I was your age, my boy, I too used to beg in the streets. I have journeyed across Spain with just a begging bowl as company. Yet, never in all my young days did I come across a beggar boy who owned such a clean handkerchief!' He passed it back, then lit the two oil lamps in the kitchen. The room was filled with yellow light and the steamed windows were black against the darkening night.

The old man wiped his sweating brow, and sat opposite the boy on a wooden chair, his watery blue eyes surveying Peter candidly. 'Alas,' he said, 'I am unable to help you. Although you may sing like an angel, I have no money here.'

'But you *can* help me,' Peter said. 'You are Sebastiano, aren't you? The great artist?'

The old man sighed, his shoulders sagging with an expression of weariness. 'No longer a great artist,' he said. 'But you are right. I am Sebastiano, my boy. Now tell me what you really want.'

'I want you to draw for me,' Peter said.

'Is that why you came? You want a drawing?'

'Yes,' Peter said. 'A drawing of yours would sell for a lot of money.'

'Enough, perhaps, to pay for the operation on your dear mother's eyes?' Sebastiano asked.

'That's right,' agreed Peter.

'You know that what you ask of me is impossible?' Sebastiano said. 'I cannot do it. Did you not know that I have vowed, ever since the death of my dear wife, never to paint or draw again? I have kept my vow, and it will never be broken.'

'But you could save my mother's sight!' Peter cried. Although he was lying to the old man, Peter felt a surge of indignation as he argued. 'Is it too much to ask for a few precious seconds of your time? Too much to ask you to scribble a few lines for my mother's sake?'

'Yes, it is too much,' said Sebastiano. 'A vow is a vow. I have sworn that there will be no more works of art from Sebastiano. Not for all the money in the world would I break this sacred oath, my boy. Not for kings, nor princes, nor for a beggar boy, even though he should own the cleanest linen handkerchief I have ever seen.'

Suddenly Sebastiano leapt from his chair, his hand touching the boy's face. 'I am an artist,' he said, 'and I know the difference between dirt which has accumulated over the months, and that which has been freshly applied to a well-scrubbed face. I know the real miseries of being a beggar, and you are indeed the most fortunate one I have ever seen in my life. Most beggars cannot afford the luxury of a barber's shop.' Peter felt the old man's fingers touch his hair. Somehow the old man was behind him now, and as he turned to face him, Sebastiano laughed aloud. Turning back towards the sound, Peter was surprised to see the old man sitting on the wooden chair before him.

At that moment he decided that he would have to try to make a break for it. The old man was far too clever to be tricked this way, and the heat in the kitchen was very uncomfortable. Peter raced for the door almost as soon as the thought had entered his head, only to be confronted by Sebastiano who had, somehow, managed to get there before him. 'Not so fast, little puppy,' said the old man. 'You have not yet answered all my questions. Why do you so desperately want one of my drawings? Eh? I presume that you are not an art collector in disguise?'

'No,' said Peter. He was frightened now. Would Sebastiano call the police?

'So why did you daub your face with mud and come here to try to trick me into drawing for you?' asked Sebastiano. 'I believe you when you tell me that you want to sell the drawing. But what did you propose buying with the money you would make?'

'A bicycle,' Peter said, his face now flushed crimson with shame. 'I wanted a bicycle for Christmas, and my father can't afford to buy one for me.'

'That you have a father is a blessing,' Sebastiano said in a not unkind voice. 'That he is unable to afford a bicycle for you is not sufficient reason for you to try to deceive an old man.'

'But its only a drawing,' said Peter. 'I reckoned that one of your drawings would sell for enough money to buy a bicycle.'

'One of my drawings would buy a hundred of those infernally dangerous contraptions!' Sebastiano cried. 'A thousand—a whole fleet of them! Not only do you try to trick me, but you insult me too!'

'I didn't mean to be rude,' said Peter. 'I just didn't know how much your drawings are worth.'

'They are worth what people will pay,' said the old man. 'A painting is worth the canvas and the materials, unless, of course, it is a masterpiece. For my part, I am only capable of producing masterpieces.'

'I didn't expect a masterpiece,' Peter told him.

'Blessed is he that expects nothing at all, for he shall never be disappointed,' Sebastiano replied.

'Are you going to report me to the police?' asked Peter fearfully.

'No,' said the old man. 'I shall teach you a lesson in my own way. I shall draw for you.'

'You're going to draw?' Peter was astounded by this sudden change of mind. 'But what about your vow?'

'My vows are my business,' said Sebastiano curtly. 'Now, do you wish me to draw, or don't you?'

'Oh, please!' said Peter.

'Then sit yourself by the oil lamp,' said the old man. 'Sit quite still and watch while I draw.'

'Thank you,' Peter replied, humbled by the old man's generosity. 'I'm sorry I tried to cheat you—honestly.'

'Honestly?' The old man smiled waspishly.

Then Sebastiano started to draw, his fingers now alive with a speed and suppleness which caused Peter to gasp aloud. 'Sit still,' the artist commanded. 'Do not move until it is finished. You will remember this day for the rest of your life, my boy, so look well and watch while I draw for you.'

Peter watched as the old man's hands moved with incredible speed, the picture growing magically, each line perfection. 'But—'

'Don't speak!' Sebastiano said sharply. 'This is my Christmas gift to you. Would you spoil it all? Would you spoil the master's gift?'

Sebastiano looked younger now, his blue eyes, once watery and weak, were like sparkling jewels. How his hands moved, his fingers dancing, skilfully, almost carelessly applying more and more lines so that Peter could now make out the shape of a head. It was a portrait! Faster-faster-lines appeared as if by magic, the old man bending and swaying, adding a touch here, a shower of lines there, not pausing for an instant to see what he had done. Now the drawing was alive, the eyes, the lips so real. Two strokes captured the expression of astonishment on the boy's face. Two more the parted lips. More lines, in rapid succession, depicted the unruly hair, and each line looked deceptively simple, yet was so precise.

Within a few seconds of starting, the portrait was finished, and the old man stood back so that Peter could see it.

Perfect.

Peter admired it, speechless, unable to move from where he sat.

'See?' cried the old man. 'I am still the master! Take it, my boy. The drawing is yours—my gift to you.'

Slowly Peter approached the drawing, his eyes fixed on those newly drawn eyes. The portrait was alive—a living, breathing thing. Then the eyes of the drawing welled up with tears, and the tears overflowed, sliding down the cheeks. Peter watched, his own eyes filling with tears. 'It's a trick!' he sobbed. 'A mean trick! Why did you draw my picture on this?' He pointed to the picture which Sebastiano had drawn, with his fingers, in the steam on the window pane of the kitchen. 'Why did you trick me?' he sobbed.

The tears trickled from the eyes of the drawing, running in thin rivulets down the cold glass, dissolving the picture, running into each other until the glass was clear and glistening wet.

This is the first time that I have found courage to relate this story, for as you may already have guessed, I was that deceitful boy. The reason for so many years of silence is that I learned some time ago that Sebastiano was dead, and had been dead for a year before my visit.

IN THE EVENING THERE WAS A BIG TRANSYLVANIAN KNEES-UP! BEFORE RETIRING TO THE CRYPT...

'Sing, Choirs of Angels . . .'

These attractive angels will make a centrepiece at Christmas to go on a table, a shelf, or round the Christmas tree. You can make them in white, silver, or gold. (For a colour photograph, see pp 34–5.)

Trace the templates on pp 156–7 on to a metallic gold or silver card, or on to plain white card. (White card can always be sprayed gold or silver, but be very careful if you do this.)

Cut a 13cm piece of florist's wire. Roll a small quantity of cotton wool around one end of the wire to look rather like a cotton-bud. Cover it with a small piece of nylon cut from old tights. Stretch it tightly and bind the ends on to the wire with sticky tape (Fig 1). This makes one hand.

Cut out the arm shapes and make them into cones by gluing along one edge. Thread the unbound end of the wire through both arm cones as shown in Fig 2. Bind the other end of the wire to make a second hand.

Make the body cone. Fix the arms, by bending the wire slightly in the middle and taping them to the back of the body cone along the joining seam. Place the back of the arms at the neck opening with three short pieces of clear sticky tape.

Make the head with cotton wool rolled smoothly into a ball about the size of a table-tennis ball.

(You can use a polystyrene ball or table-tennis ball if you have them.) Cut a piece of nylon from a pair of old tights. Stretch this over the head shape, tying the gathers tightly with thread at the bottom to form a neck (Fig 3).

You can use white Christmas floss to make the angels' hair, but strands of wool would do just as well. Tie the strands in the middle of a number of 25cm lengths to make a parting. Glue the hair to the head and arrange a hair style, using small amounts of

glue applied with a cocktail stick to hold it in place.

Use blue or black map pins for eyes. But if you like, you can simply paint the eyes on.

Take a doily and cut a small cross in the centre. Holding the head carefully in one hand, push the neck gathers through the centre of the doily. Put glue around the gathers and push the neck into the opening of the body cone. Put one hand up inside the body cone from the bottom and gently pull the neck nylon tight. Press it against the cone and hold it until the glue is dry and firm. Now arrange the doily over the arms.

The three glue flaps should be folded outward. Put glue on top of the flaps and press the body cone down on the base, holding it in place until the glue has set.

Chester Carol

He who made the earth so fair
Slumbers in a stable bare,
Warmed by cattle standing there.

Oxen, lowing, stand all round;
In the stall no other sound
Mars the peace by Mary found.

Joseph piles the soft, sweet hay,
Starlight drives the dark away,
Angels sing a heavenly lay.

Jesus sleeps in Mary's arm;
Sheltered there from rude alarm,
None can do Him ill or harm.

See His mother o'er Him bend;
Hers the joy to soothe and tend,
Hers the bliss that knows no end.

A Peculiar Christmas

Snow? Absolutely not.
In fact, the weather's quite hot.
At night you can watch this new
Star without catching the 'flu.

Presents? Well, only three.
But then there happen to be
Only three guests. No bells,
No robins, no fir-trees, no smells

—I mean of roast turkey and such:
There are whiffs in the air (a bit much!)
Of beer from the near public-house,
And of dirty old shepherds, and cows.

The family party's rather
Small—baby, mother and father—
Uncles, aunts, cousins dispersed.
Well, this Christmas *is* only the first.

Penelope's Carol

Christmas Time

This carol was written by Penelope Hughes when she was 8 years old.
It won first prize in the 1980 Bach Choir competition and was performed
in the Royal Albert Hall.

Al - le - lu - ia, al - le - lu - ia, al - le - lu - ia.

Fine

Interlude (between verses)

D.S.

The Story of Prudence Trigg

Prudence Trigg, with Christmas near,
Said one evening: 'Mummy, dear,
A Christmas stocking and a tree
Just don't mean a thing to me.
And while those books and paints and toys
Are fine for other girls and boys,
I've had enough, and any more
Would just become a frightful bore.'

Said Mrs Trigg: 'Dear, when you speak,
I wish you wouldn't grunt and squeak.
Please talk as you're supposed to do,
And not like something from the zoo.'

But spoilt Prudence shook her head.
'Do pay attention, Mum,' she said.
'You see, I only want three things—
And not the stuff that Santa brings.

First of all—a special treat:
Lots of lovely things to eat.
And then a party dress in blue,
With satin sleeves—a bow or two—
And lots of frills, and—let me think—
A silky sash of damask pink.'
And, when she had described her frock,
She grunted: 'Then, at four o'clock,
I'd like a party, just for me,
So I can ask my friends to tea.'

'But, dear', said Mrs Trigg, poor soul,
'We've sent a letter to the Pole.
We've made a list of everything
We wanted Santa Clause to bring.
He will be sad if, after all,
We have to tell him not to call.
I only hope he'll understand,
With all his nice surprises planned.'

'Let him keep them!' Prudence said.
'I've told you what I want instead!'

So Mrs Trigg took out her pen
To write to Santa there and then.
With blots and crossings-out she wrote:
'Do please excuse this hurried note,
But I've a headache fit for two,
All brought on by my daughter, Prue.
I have to tell you not to call.
She says she wants no toys at all,
But just three things—no more, no less:
A party, food and party-dress.

'I must close now—my headache's worse—'
(She always wrote her notes in verse)
'—With love to you and Mrs C.—
Your sincerely, Mrs T.'

On Christmas Eve, Prue went to bed,
With thoughts a-buzzing in her head
Of all the lovely things she'd eat
Tomorrow morning—what a treat!
And what a party there would be
When all her friends came round for tea.
And how they'd OH! and AH! and OOOH!
When they saw her dress of blue.

When morning came, downstairs she saw
The things that she'd been hoping for:
A really lovely party-dress,
And, all around the room, no less
Than five big tables, each spread out
With all the food she'd dreamed about.

And while she stood there, all excited,
Mrs Trigg said, 'I've invited
All your friends—yes, every one—
To play some games and have some fun.'
Prue just grunted: 'Well, that's fine,
But till they come the food's all mine.'
And, cutting off a slice of meat,
She sat down and commenced to eat.

Beef and chicken, pork and lamb,
Salad-rolls and eggs and ham,
Jelly, cakes and marmalade—
What a spectacle she made!
As if she couldn't get enough,
Hour by hour she sat and stuffed
Herself with everything she could.
And when she'd done, she snorted: 'Good—
I'll go upstairs and have a rest
Before it's time to greet my guests.'

She woke again at half-past three
And said: 'There's something wrong with me.
I don't feel well. I feel half dead.
There's such a pounding in my head.
And in my tummy such a pain,
I swear I'll never eat again!'

Then Mrs Trigg knocked on the door
And called: 'My dear, it's nearly four!'
So Prue took down her party-frock
To put it on—but what a shock—
She found that she had scoffed too much
Of all that cake and meat and such,
And now she saw to her surprise
That she had swelled up twice the size!
Her lovely dress just would not fit,
For she'd grown much too fat for it.

Prue's friends had such a lovely time
And played their games till almost nine,
While she stayed in her room alone,
Too ill to do much more than groan.

Her mother said, the children gone:
'I'll see how Prue is getting on.'
But what a horror! What a sight!
Had little Prue become that night!
Her mother found her on the bed,
The party dress jammed on her head,
All tattered now like bits of bunting
As she lay there slowly grunting,
Squinting up her sow-like eyes
At her mother's anguished cries.
Poor Mrs T. just stood and wailed—
Her daughter now was curly-tailed!

Although it's true, it's sad to say
That Prue changed from a child that day.
And from that moment Prudence Trigg
Was always known as Prudence Pig.

A Victorian Christmas Tree

I can hardly describe the scene that met my sight. The room was brilliantly lighted up with coloured lamps hanging from the ceiling and the walls, and gaily festooned with green leaves and coronets of holly-berries and mistletoe. There was no furniture in the room, but in the centre, on the floor, there was placed a gigantic Christmas Tree, whose topmost branches almost reached the ceiling. It was loaded with toys and presents, and dazzling with light which proceeded from a multitude of little tapers hung about among the dark fir branches in all directions. Little numerous glass globes, sparkling with various metallic colours, that made them look like balls of gold and silver, added to the beautiful effect.

The company, especially the children, were astonished at the beauty of the Christmas Tree, and were loud in its praises; and presently, some musicians in the next room striking up a merry tune, all men, women and children—commenced searching about among the branches for the toys and presents that bore their names. Such shouting and laughing, and singing and scrambling, and giggling and romping; such merry noise, and innocent, light-hearted gaiety; such joking, and quizzing, and bantering, as there was, as each one found the toy intended for him—I cannot describe for the life of me. I only know that for an hour or more the fun continued, till nearly every one in the room had possession of a bon-bon in gilt paper, or a toy watch, or a box of crackers, or something of that kind. There were sugar-frosted fruits and sweetmeats, with mottoes slyly concealed inside, for the ladies and gentlemen; and little dolls, and little tops, and little coloured balls, and all kinds of toys and confectionery for the boys and girls, with numerous other things for which I can find no names. And the romps grew loud and gay as the minutes passed.

The Christmas Tree

Put out the lights now!
Look at the Tree, the rough tree dazzled
In oriole plumes of flame,
Tinselled with twinkling frost fire, tassled
With stars and moons—the same
That yesterday hid in the spinney
    and had no fame
Till we put out the lights now.

Hard are the nights now;
The fields at moonrise turn to agate,
Shadows are cold as jet:
In dyke and furrow, in copse and faggot
The frost's tooth is set;
And stars are the sparks whirled
    by the north wind's fret
On the flinty nights now.

So feast your eyes now
On mimic star and moon-cold bauble:
Worlds may wither unseen,
But the Christmas Tree is a tree of fable.
A phoenix in evergreen,
And the world cannot change or chill
    what its mysteries mean
To your hearts and eyes now.

The vision dies now
Candle by candle: the tree that embraced it
Returns to its own kind,
To be earthed again and weather as best it
May the frost and wind.
Children, it too had its hour—
    you will not mind
If it lives or dies now.

Horace's Christmas Disappointment

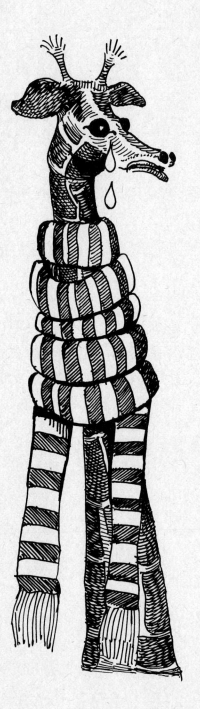

Young Horace Giraffe on Christmas Eve
Put out his stocking to receive
Whatever Santa Claus might bring.
You may indeed be wondering
What sort of size such stockings are,
Since even small giraffes are far
Bigger than quite a tall man is.
Young Horace Giraffe had measured his,
And found it stretched four feet or so
From ample top to roomy toe.

What piles and piles of presents he
Imagined packed there presently!
A hundred tangerines; a bunch
Of ripe bananas for his lunch;
Five watermelons; fifty figs;
The most delicious juicy sprigs
Plucked from the tops of special trees
With leaves as sweet as honey-bees;
And in the very bottom, some
Chocolates full of candied rum.

Alas, poor Horace! Christmas Day
Dawned, and he rose from where he lay
To snatch the stocking from the bed—
But though it bulged, he felt with dread
How light it was . . . He reached inside—
And then he very nearly died.

Inside the stocking, almost half
The size of Horace, was a SCARF
(A useful garment, yes, I know,
But oh, it was a bitter blow.)
The scarf was fully ten yards long,
And striped and bright and very strong.
It filled the stocking, top to toe,
And Horace was quite filled with woe.

The moral is: A *USEFUL* PRESENT
IN STOCKINGS IS RATHER
SELDOM PLEASANT.

Pass the Angel

This game, for any number of players, is fun to play. The rules are simple, but winning is tantalisingly difficult!

You will need
different coloured small counters for each player and one die.

TO PLAY:
Each player throws the die and places his counter on the same number on the tree. Players then throw the die in turn, and move their counters the number of spaces indicated by the die.

PENALTIES:
1. If a player's counter lands on any space number 1–12 which is already occupied by an opponent, it must go back to the beginning.

2. Once past the angel, however, a counter which lands on an occupied space need only move back two spaces. Should that space be occupied, it must go back a further two spaces.

3. If an opponent's counter is on spaces 14 or 15 and the player thus has to retreat to the angel or to space 12, the player must go back to the start. If an advancing player lands on space 12 or on the angel, he must also return to the start.

4. If a player's counter lands on space 25 it must retreat to space 14.

END OF PLAY
The winner is the first one whose throw gets him past 25 and into home.

113

Egg Decorations

Various countries have devised their own special types of Christmas tree decorations. None was as elaborate and beautiful as the intricate scenes that hung on German trees a hundred years ago. Made of paper, straw, shells and apple peel, each was a work of art in itself. Why not add something special to your tree by making these beautiful egg decorations?

Any egg will do—a chicken's egg, a duck's egg, or a goose's egg. Larger eggs give more room inside for winter scenes, little figures, or dried flower arrangements.

Draw a window on the side of your chosen egg with pencil or crayon.

Make a small hole with a darning needle.

Use very fine, sharp scissors (fingernail or embroidery scissors) and cut carefully round the window you have drawn.

Lift the piece of shell away carefully and empty the contents of the egg into a bowl. Rinse the shell and let it dry.

If you are going to make a number of these decorations you may need a drying rack. For this take a piece of wood about 5cm thick. Hammer in some long, thin nails 5 to 8cm apart so that you can hang the eggs on the nails, and they will not touch each other.

The eggs can now be coloured. Paint them with food colouring, lacquer, fingernail polish, or acrylic paint. Perhaps the quickest and most effective method is to glue on thin coloured foil saved from toffees, chocolates, or certain wrapped biscuits.

Decorate the outside of the egg with beads saved from old necklaces, old discarded ear-rings, ribbons, sequins, cording, buttons, lace, dried flowers, pieces cut from gold doilys, or pasta pieces or shapes, sprayed with gold paint.

Start by putting a frame of pearls, small beads, or pretty cord round the opening with a clear all-purpose glue. It is easier to glue pearls or beads if they remain on a string while you work. You can then cut the string when you know exactly how many you need.

For a hanger you will need a 25cm length of cord ribbon, thin wire, or fishing line. If you have a metal filigree bell-cap, knot and thread the cord through it before you glue it to the top of the egg.

Now use your imagination to make patterns around the egg-shell, and gently put it aside to dry.

If you want a snow scene, carefully brush wallpaper paste all over the inside and coat it with glitter or Epsom Salts. Choose what you want to put inside your egg. You may like to cut out a scene from a Christmas card, or you might like to put little figures. For this use Christmas cake decorations or little dolls or animals. If you have any dried flowers, you can make a pretty arrangement with these.

To make a shelf inside the bottom of the egg for your figures or snow scene, beat half a cup of washing-powder with a tablespoon of water into a paste until it looks like snow. Fill the bottom of the egg carefully so that the paste is just below the bottom of the opening. Push figures, the winter scene, or dried flowers gently into the paste. Tweezers will help to get small things through the tiny opening into just the right place. When the paste dries, the miniatures will be held quite firmly.

A Christmas Letter from Italy

Dear Hans,

How do you spend your Christmas Holiday? I always enjoy mine very much. A week before Christmas I start to decorate my house with glittering ribbons and greetings posters. As usual, I prepare the crèche (*il presepe*) in a corner of the living room. Next to the crèche I put the Christmas tree. I enjoy hanging up the beautiful decorations—the angels, the lights, the star on the top.

Father Christmas brings us our presents. I find mine under the tree on Christmas morning. I always wonder if I have been good enough during the year to deserve the presents. My mother told me that, when she was a little girl, it was Gesu Bambino (Baby Jesus) who brought the presents, and all the children used to write letters to Him promising to be good.

We go to midnight Mass on Christmas Eve, and in the church there is a huge crèche with figures about half a metre high.

On Christmas Day we don't have a special dinner but there is a rich lunch with some special cakes such as *il panettone, il pandoro* and *il torrone*, and then we finish off with *la frutta secca*.

We are lucky in Italy, because after Christmas we have another festivity called la Befana. La Befana is a nice little old lady who brings sweets to every good child and some coal to naughty children. (The coal is really a sweet that looks like coal!) La Befana flies from house to house on her broomstick on the night of Epiphany and puts her gifts in socks which we hang by the chimney before going to bed.

Buon Natale Felice,
Anno Nuovo!
Paolo

A Christmas Letter from Holland

Dear Paolo,

I've just come back from the town. There are so many people there all trying to buy their presents. Inside the shops there are real Father Christmases who take the toddlers on their laps. Floop! A photograph. Just the same as with St Nicholas.

I came back with the Christmas tree. In a little while I'm going to decorate it with paper chains, balls, little wreaths called *kransjes*, bells, angels, and on the top a really beautiful glass ornament called a *piek*.

In Holland you will find candles and lights in every home. They are lit on 24th and 25th of December. Mother has wrapped up the presents and she's put them under the Christmas tree, but we aren't allowed to open them until Christmas Day.

Now mother is busy in the kitchen making *kersttulband*, a round cake with a hole in the middle. On the 23rd she makes the first preparations for the Christmas dinner. On the 24th she'll still have enough to do cooking the turkey or chicken and preparing the fruit salad and all the vegetables.

That evening our friends and family will sit round the table for the dinner. There will be at least fifteen of us. We all bring our presents but put them under the tree. Later in the evening they will be given out over a few drinks. At midnight we will go to the Christmas service.

On Christmas morning we have a special breakfast; a kind of fruit loaf called *kerstbrood*. Mother has an easier time if there is food left over from the previous evening.

On the 26th of December all the decorations are put away again, and the tree is put outside the front door. It is taken away by children, who burn it together with many other trees in the fields that same evening. That is regarded as the end of Christmas by everyone, and we start to think about the New Year.

But on the 6th of January we dress up as the Three Kings and ring the doorbells in the street. We sing a song and get some fruit or biscuits. On that day we also eat a big cake which mother bakes and in which she hides a bean. Whoever gets the bean is prince or princess and is allowed to choose his favourite meal for the next day.

That is the end of the celebrations. The nicest time of the year.

Prettige Kerstdagen
en een gelukkig Nieuwyaar,
Hans

Christmas in the Castle

During the Christmas of 1507, Edward Stafford the Duke of Buckingham held a magnificent Christmas celebration at Thornbury Castle in Gloucestershire. Throughout the twelve days, he provided lavish hospitality and gave a number of splendid banquets.

The last banquet of the holiday, held on the Feast of the Epiphany (6 January), was the most magnificent of all, when 459 people sat down to dine. Not only were there 134 noblemen and gentry with all their attendants, but there were such guests as the local abbot, the doctor, the chaplain, a hermit, a brickmaker and a joiner.

Extra cooks were brought in from Bristol to help prepare the feast, and the Duke hired a number of musicians and singers to entertain his guests.

A household book was kept by the Duke's secretary, in which all provisions for the feast were noted down. This included every item of food and drink that was consumed. It even listed the number of tapers and candles, as well as the quantity of hay provided for the horses of the guests.

Here is a list of items
provided at the Duke's feast:

36 rounds of beef	100 lampreys
12 carcases of mutton	200 oysters
2 calves	½ fresh salmon
4 pigs	1 fresh cod
6 suckling pigs	1 salt sturgeon
2 lambs	21 roach
22 rabbits	4 dog-fish
3 swans	10 little whiting
6 geese	½ fresh conger
2 peacocks	17 flounders
2 herons	2 tench
18 chickens	3 plaice
16 woodcock	7 little bream
20 snipe	6 large eels
10 capons	400 eggs
108 great birds	24 dishes of butter
72 little birds	3 flagons of cream
36 larks	15 flagons of milk
9 quail	2 gallons of frumety
9 mallard	259 flagons (gallons) of ale
23 wigeon	several gallons of four
18 teal	different kinds of wine

Pantomime

Girls dressed as boys, men playing women, people throwing custard pies at each other, a fairy tale laced with music—where did this peculiarly British form of entertainment come from?

The ancient Romans had something similar, but the first elements of what we now know as pantomime stems from an Italian form of theatre called the commedia dell' arte. This was a sixteenth-century tradition of comedies performed by groups of actors who travelled all over Italy. They spoke mainly improvised dialogue and acted the parts of comic characters called Harlequin, Columbine, Pantaloon, and Clown.

The comedies were very popular and spread to other countries, where they became known as the Harlequinade, named after the main character, Harlequin. Travelling actors brought the Harlequinades to Paris and then to London, where they were performed in theatres. By 1815 theatre managers were putting on very elaborate Harlequinades in London, mainly on classical themes, but still featuring the traditional characters of Harlequin and Columbine.

Classical mythology went out of fashion at the end of the nineteenth century, and popular fairy tales were worked into traditional Harlequinades. Pantomimes then had names such as *Harlequin and Cinderella* and *Harlequin and the Giant-Killer*. Eventually the Harlequinade characters disappeared completely from pantomimes, and a new tradition was brought in from the Victorian music hall. Variety artists flooded into pantomimes, bringing with them popular songs and topical jokes, together with a great deal of clowning. From the stories of Charles Perrault, a seventeenth-century French author, popular writers devised *Cinderella*, *Sleeping Beauty*, and *Puss in Boots*. From the *Arabian Nights* we are introduced to *Aladdin*, *Sinbad the Sailor*, and *Ali Baba*. *Babes in the Wood* comes from a fifteenth-century legend, which sets the story in Waylands Wood in Norfolk. *Dick Whittington* was a real man who was in fact thrice Lord Mayor of London. But he wasn't poor, he didn't hear any bells, and he didn't own a cat.

All the stories in fact were changed, and are still changing. The first performance of Cinderella was on Boxing Day 1860. The cast included Baron Balderdash, his daughters Corinda and Thisbe, and someone called Buttoni—the original Buttons. *Aladdin* first appeared in 1861 in a burlesque form. Aladdin's mother was called Widow Twankey, at a time when tea-clippers raced home from China with cargoes of twankey—a variety of green tea.

The leading comic character is the Dame:

Dame Trot, Mother Goose, the Ugly Sisters. The tradition of a man playing a woman goes back to the Greeks and Romans. In Elizabethan plays men or boys always played women's parts. The Dame first became established in pantomime in the 1860s, and was usually played by a music-hall comedian. Nowadays dames are often television stars. One of the greatest dames was Dan Leno. When he died, his funeral route was three and a half miles long and was lined with people three deep.

The tradition of women playing men is not so old. It started in the eighteenth century, but by the 1880s it was quite usual in pantomimes. Nowadays young comedians or television stars often play the hero's part.

Present-day pantomimes are still as popular and as lavish as the old Victorian ones. They still have transformation scenes, waterfalls, real horses, and very large casts. They traditionally open on Boxing Day and play for 2–3 months. Whether they are lavish or modest, they all end with the grand finale: virtue is rewarded, evil is punished, and the lovers live happily ever after.

Decorations you can Eat

Biscuit tree ornaments

First trace the shapes you want to use from the templates inside the front and back covers of the book. Cut the patterns out of cardboard. It is a good idea to cover these stencils with kitchen foil.

To make the icing you will need:
2 standard size egg whites
1lb (450g) of icing sugar
1 teaspoon of almond flavouring
2 tablespoons of water

To make the biscuits you will need:
1lb (450g) of plain flour
1lb (450g) sugar
1 teaspoon of bicarbonate of soda
½ teaspoon of salt
4oz (120g) butter
2 eggs
4 tablespoons top of milk or single cream
1 teaspoon almond flavouring
1 teaspoon vanilla essence
finely grated rind of 1 orange

Sift the flour, sugar, bicarbonate of soda and salt into a bowl. Rub in the butter with your fingers until the mixture looks like bread crumbs. Beat the eggs, cream, orange rind, almond, and vanilla together. Add this to the dry ingredients and mix well. Roll out the dough on a lightly floured board. Then lay the foil-covered shapes on top, and cut out carefully with a knife. The shaded circle on the template shows where to make the hole for the ribbon with which you will hang the biscuits from the tree.

Remember this hole will get smaller as the biscuit bakes, so be sure to make it large enough.

Take up the shapes carefully with a spatula or slice, and place them on a greased baking sheet. Bake for 10 minutes at 350 F (180 C), gas mark 4. When they are lightly brown, remove and cool before icing them.

Now make the icing:
Beat the icing until it stands up in peaks. Put in several small bowls and add a different food colouring for each so that you have a palette of colours with which to decorate your biscuits.

In addition you can use melted chocolate, 'hundreds and thousands', dried flowers, or any cake decorations.

You can paint directly onto white icing with food colouring and a fine brush.

When you have finished, leave the icing to harden. Then thread a 30cm piece of ribbon through the hole and tie it into a bow, ready to hang from the Christmas tree branches.

Popcorn Snowballs

To pop a packet of popcorn, pour a small amount of cooking oil in a large saucepan with a tightly fitting lid. Sprinkle enough popcorn kernels into the pan to cover the surface of the bottom. Put the lid on and replace the pan on a fairly hot cooker ring. Shake the pan from time to time to prevent burning and listen for the popping corn. Do not take off the lid until the popping has finished.

To make the snowballs, you will need about 20 teacupfuls of popped corn. Keep the corn hot and crisp in a slow oven while you do the rest of the popping. Butter the sides of a saucepan and put in 1lb (2 cups) of sugar, ½ teaspoon of salt, and ½ teaspoon of vinegar. Cook until it forms a hard ball when a little is dropped from a spoon into cold water. Remove the pan from the heat and add 1 teaspoon of vanilla. Pour this syrup slowly over the hot popped corn, mixing well to coat every kernel. Press into small round balls. Butter your hands lightly if necessary.

Wrap each ball in a square of plastic wrap, and tie a piece of ribbon around the top. These balls can be hung from the Christmas tree branches or strung with a bodkin, threaded with ribbon to make a garland.

Jellydrop stars

You will need large and small jellydrops, cocktail sticks, and long hairpins.

Push eight cocktail sticks around a large jellydrop and a ninth one in the centre. Add small jellydrops in a variety of colours to the end of the cocktail sticks. Push the ends of a long hairpin into the centre of the large jellydrop as a hanger to slip over the ends of the tree branches.

Polo Chain

Cut two pieces of gold cord slightly longer than you want your chain to be. The trick is to get the sweets to lie flat. This is done by weaving the two cords in and out over alternate sides of each ring. It takes about three rolls of sweets to make one metre of sweet chain.

Marshmallow garland

With a sharp knife cut a roll of cling film into three sections to form ribbons, each about 10cm wide. Stretch out the ribbon and place marshmallows every five cm.

Twist the plastic ribbon and secure the sections between the marshmallows with strips of coloured or metallic tape.

The Father Christmas Biscuit

Use the five-pointed star template on page 158 to make Father Christmas decorations. Cut out a pattern to the size you want and cover with kitchen foil. Roll out your biscuit dough and cut out the star-shapes. Place carefully on a baking tray. Twist the top point slightly to the right for the cap and turn the two bottom points up slighly for the feet (Fig 1).

through the hole in his hat, and Father Christmas is ready to hang from the tree.

Make a hole in the top point if you wish to hang them from the tree. Bake and remove carefully from the baking sheets and cool. Put red icing on the body and pink on the face (Fig 2). Then trim with white icing for fur and beard. Melt chocolate over hot water and use this for boots and gloves. When the icing has set, put a ribbon

Hint:
If you want your biscuit decorations to hang with the icing to the front, take a 40cm length of ribbon, fold it in half, and push the fold through the hole. Pull this loop up behind far enough (Fig 3) to put the two ends through. Tie the ends over the branch in a bow.

Christmas in Australia

Christmas in Australia is an out-of-doors festival. The hottest month of the Australian summer is February, but even so there are heat-waves in December and January with the temperatures ranging between 30–40°C.

Despite the heat, none of the meaning of Christmas is lost. All the seasonal celebrations are observed. Homes and gardens (or yards) are decorated with greenery, Christmas trees, and fairy lights. And in sunshine hot enough to start bush-fires raging, windows can be seen sprayed with artificial snow, flaming puddings are served, and at children's parties even a perspiring Santa Claus can be found.

Australian children like to look out for what they call the 'Christmas' beetle. This is an insect about 2cm long with a black underside and an orange decoration on its back. This clumsy slow-flying creature appears at Christmas time and bangs into windows or clings to clothes.

Seasonal plants are the Christmas bush—a shrub with hazy clusters of tiny reddish flowers; and the Christmas bell—a bell-shaped flower with a bright green stamen.

Most families make for the beaches or parks on Christmas Day. For dinner they enjoy cold turkey, chicken, or ham with cold vegetables and salad.

Before Christmas, large numbers of people gather in the many parks for candlelit carol services. Such huge gatherings in the warmth of a summer's evening, as thousands of voices unite and rejoice, have become a unique and moving part of an Australian Christmas.

A Christmas Letter from Australia

Dear Mandy,

I hope you had a happy Christmas. This year we spent our holiday at Eden in a friend's house, which they lent us for three weeks. Luckily we don't have to go back to school until the beginning of February as we are now in our summer holidays. While we were in Eden we went down to the beach every day and the sea was lovely and refreshing. On Christmas day it was too hot to go down to the beach until after lunch. So at about 9.30 we went to a Christmas service in a tiny church. As we walked home we disturbed a brown snake sunning itself in the dust.

Lunch was cold, thank goodness! Turkey, ham, salad, and ice-cream Christmas pudding with glacé fruit—YUM!

What did you get for Christmas? I got two peaked sun-hats from Mum and Dad; one pink and one orange and they are really nice. Grandad and Grandma gave me a pair of shorts and a T-shirt.

We met all our friends down at the beach for a barbecue tea. We had to be careful of the blue-bottle jelly fish, as they covered the sand below the high-tide mark. It was a hot evening and the cicadas were very noisy. After tea, we all went beachcombing, collecting interesting shells and stone. I found a stone with a hole through the middle, which is supposed to be lucky. When it gets cooler in the evening the millions of pestering flies settle down, then all the mosquitoes come out!

Our Christmas tree became dried out very quickly and all its needles fell off!

I'd love to hear about a white Christmas, so please write soon.

Love from
Leanne

Away in a Manger

All over the world, just before Christmas, in homes, churches, town squares and market places people set up the Christmas crèche to recreate the Nativity.

Children stand and gaze in at the model figures of the Holy Family in the stable at Bethlehem as the animals stand by and watch and the shepherds kneel in adoration.

In a Munich Square, after a heavy fall of snow, passers-by watch as a snow-crèche is built.

In Amalfi, in southern Italy, under the water of the Emerald Grotto, fishermen place on the sea-floor a crèche with life-size pottery figures.

In the window of a large department store in New York is a 'space-crèche', showing a Martian setting with the three kings arriving by space capsule.

In the corner of the hall in a village school in the north of England, pupils put the finishing touches to their papier mâché Nativity figures, whose stable has been made out of a large cardboard egg box.

Just as the Christmas tree is the centre piece of the Christmas observances in homes and churches in northern Europe, so in southern Europe Christmas is centred around the crèche.

In Italy the crèche or *presepio* is especially well-loved. In almost every home it is caringly set up and the Christmas gifts are placed in front of it. During the twelve days of Christmas candles are lit, and these throw their warm light on to the still figures of the Nativity within.

On Christmas Eve the family gathers round the scene. The manger is empty. The family kneels before the *presepio* and sing carols. The next morning the Baby Jesus is placed in his manger in a special ceremony.

Over Christmas, Italian families will go visiting to view the crèches in their friends' homes.

French children also love the crèche. For them too it is the chief feature of their Christmas festivity.

Often a French crèche will include figures

Italian crèche

Tahitian crèche

French crèche from Provence.

not directly connected with the Nativity. These figures are called *santons*, or 'little saints'.

Each December, in Marseilles, a crèche fair is held where *santons* and other crèche figures are sold.

Like the Italians, many French families celebrate Christmas round the crèche. In some parts of France, it is a custom for children to make their own small manger scenes in cardboard boxes which they take round to show neighbours. If the children sing carols they are rewarded with small gifts.

The very first crèche was created in 1224 by St Francis of Assisi. One evening he saw some shepherds lying asleep in the fields near the little town of Greccio. The scene reminded him so strongly of the shepherds in the Christmas story that he was inspired by the idea of making a nativity scene so that ordinary peasant folk could understand more fully the beauty and simplicity of the Holy Birth.

St Francis put the crèche in a forest grotto with a real ox and ass tethered inside. He placed a life-size wax figure of the Christ Child in the manger, and real people represented Joseph, Mary, and the shepherds.

On Christmas Eve crowds of people from surrounding villages flocked to celebrate mass around the crèche. They carried lighted tapers and sang hymns. A legend says that as St Francis spoke of the Babe lying in the manger, the sky seemed to glow, and the crèche was bathed in a bright light.

After this the nativity scene was recreated every year at Greccio, and soon the idea spread to other towns in Italy. Gradually the custom spread to other countries—especially to France, Spain, Portugal, and Southern Germany. In these countries the making of crèche figures is a craft which is cherished and is handed down from generation to generation.

The Boar's Head

For many centuries, a wild boar's head, roasted or boiled, was considered to be a great delicacy. By the middle part of the Middle ages there were fewer and fewer boars, and so the dish became something of a rarity. It was eaten in the halls of royalty, nobility, or gentry on special occasions. At Christmas time it was carried to the table with great ceremony. It would be decorated with garlands of laurel, bay, and rosemary, and in its mouth would be an orange or a lemon.

At Queen's College, Oxford, the boar's head ceremony continues. The head is made of jellied meats pressed into a mould and it is carried in by three bearers. Ahead of it walk trumpeters and the choir who sing the Boar's Head Carol:

> The Boar's Head in hand bear I,
> Bedeck'd with bays and rosemary,
> And I pray you, my masters, be merry,
> *Quot estis in convivio.*

The ceremony is said to have been started by one of the students at the college. One day he was walking in Shotover forest deeply engrossed in reading a book. Suddenly a wild boar rushed out and attacked him. The student had no time to draw his sword, so he rammed his book down the boar's throat and it choked to death. He then cut off the head and carried it back to the college in triumph.

Christmas Crossword

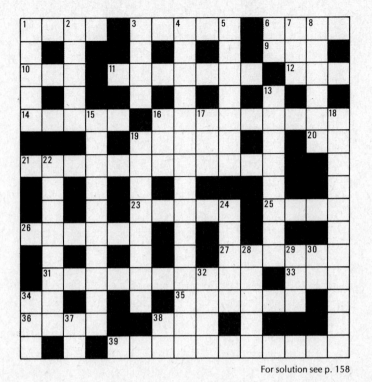

For solution see p. 158

Across

1. Wise men from the East (4)
3. They should be well wrapped up at Christmas time (5)
6. 'Following yonder ____' (4)
9. Toes tangled in net? (3)
10. Rather a strange Christmas spirit in the butter (3)
11. The shine you can buy in a packet (7)
12. Eaten (all or part) (3)
14. Large numbers of angels (5)
16. Birthplace of the Holy Child (9)
19. French for Mary (5)
20. Not your (2)
21. Cefranknse, a gift for Christmas! (12)
23. Girl singing at Christmas (5)
25. 'The Heavenly ____ you there shall find' (4)
26. Play ball! Jump for joy! (6)
27. Which country gave the tree? Ray won, cleverly (6)
31. Ben Hur was one, once (10)

33. Mountain to ski down, pal, out of control (3)
34. '____ came down to earth from heaven' (2)
35. Manager has lost his heart in the stall (6)
36. The first man (4)
38. Fathers—would they take this step in ballet? (3)
39. Where Joseph of Arimathea landed and planted his staff (11)

Down

1. The third gift of the wise men (5)
2. They're played at parties (5)
3. Did Caspar go prospecting for this? (4)
4. Who's red and jolly and comes out at night? (6, 9)
6. & 5. His feast is on 26 December (2, 7)
7. You can eat or drink it (3)
8. A song of praise and joy (6)
13. The last of the twelve (8)

15. German Christmas tree (10)
16. Forbid a banana split? (3)
17. A present for Dad? (3)
18. Isn't it strange to find no detectives in this performance? (7, 4)
19. Meat isn't really the filling for it (5-3)
22. 'They ____ with exceeding great joy' (8)
24. Lenin is crumpled like Irish tea-towels! (5)
28. Groan horribly, it's piped music! (5)
29. Opposite of peace (3)
30. ____ Capone (2)
32. Turn round seat towards sunrise (4)
34. Bad acting! Where are the eggs? (3)
37. How a Yuletide starts, always (2)
38. Papa's shrunk! Maybe he's lost his other half (2)

129

The story of 'Silent Night'

The words of the beautiful carol 'Silent Night' were written in 1818 by Father Joseph Mohr, who was the assistant pastor of the church of St Nicholas in the small town of Oberndorf in the Austrian Tyrol.

Late one afternoon, just before Christmas, Joseph Mohr was called out to bless a new-born baby. As he walked home through the snow, Father Mohr was deeply impressed by the beauty of the starlit night. He thought of the tiny baby he had just visited. He wondered: was it on a night of such peace and stillness that the Holy Babe was born? When he reached his house he put his feelings into words and wrote a poem.

On the day before Christmas Eve it was discovered that mice had eaten the organ bellows and put the church organ out of action. The organ builder lived in Zillertal and could not get through the snow in time to repair the damage. What could be done about the music for the Christmas service? Father Mohr thought of his poem and showed it to his friend Franz Gruber, the church choirmaster. Franz took the poem home and, within an hour, had written a simple tune.

Everyone was delighted with it. And that Christmas Eve, it was sung by Franz, Joseph and two women singers, with Joseph accompanying on his guitar.

After Christmas when the organ builder came to repair the organ, Franz Gruber played the song on the organ. The organ builder was enchanted with it and asked if he could write down the words and music and play the song at his church at Zillertal.

Soon the beautiful carol was a favourite among the churchgoers of Zillertal. They called it 'The Song from Heaven'.

Gradually the song made its way to Leipzig where it was heard by the city's Director of Music, who included it in a concert played before the Queen of Saxony. The Queen requested that it should be played in the palace on Christmas Eve 1832 so that her children could learn it.

In 1840, 'Silent Night' was published in Leipzig but it was called 'A Tyrolean Christmas Carol'. Its popularity began to spread through Europe. Still no one knew who had written the words and music. It was published again as a four-part song with the 'author and composer unknown'. Some people believed it had been written by Michael and Joseph Haydn.

In 1854 the King of Prussia, Frederick Wilhelm IV, heard the song performed by the entire choir of the Imperial Church in Berlin. Immediately he declared that the song was to be sung at all Christmas concerts in his country that Christmas. He ordered his musicians to find out who had composed such beautiful music.

Some time after this Franz Gruber's son heard about the song and recognized it as his father's music. After thirty-six years the carol that was loved by millions of people came back to the two men who had written it.

The Thorn and The Rose

The Glastonbury Thorn

Every year a spray is cut from the famous Glastonbury thorn and sent to the Queen for the royal table on Christmas Day. The thorn blossoms at Christmas time. The legend behind the custom goes back to Joseph of Arimathea, who lived at the time of Jesus and was one of his followers.

Shortly after the Crucifixion, Joseph of Arimathea came as a Christian missionary to Glastonbury to found a church there. He arrived by ship, for in those days the hills of Somerset formed an island. After Joseph and his followers had landed, they set off inland until they came to a hill. Being weary, they stopped to rest. This hill became known as Weary-All Hill.

Joseph had a thorn staff with him and he stuck it in the ground. The staff immediately took root and blossomed. After that the thorn blossomed every year—in May and again at Christmas time.

The original tree grew to an enormous size, and as it grew it divided. A Puritan, during the rule of Oliver Cromwell, considering the tree to be idolatrous, tried to cut it down. He succeeded in felling one half, but as he cut into the other, a chip of wood flew out and blinded him. A few years later the remaining part of the tree died, but cuttings had been taken. These are still growing in many places, including the ruins of Glastonbury Abbey and in the churchyard.

Up until the time of Charles I, it was the custom for a sprig of the tree to be sent to the reigning monarch. The custom was continued in the first half of this century.

The Christmas Rose

The Christmas rose, or *Helleborus niger*, is one of the few plants to bloom in the winter time. It is an attractive plant with white or whitish-pink flowers.

The black root of the plant was once thought to have considerable medicinal properties. It was also believed that it would ward off evil spirits. For this reason it was often to be found in the gardens of country cottages.

The Goose is Getting Fat

Gertrude was a goose like any other goose. Hatched out in the orchard one drizzly morning in June, she spent those early weeks looking at the world from the warm sanctuary of her mother's all-enveloping softness. It might have come as a surprise to her to know that her mother was not a goose. Of course Gertrude was convinced she was, and that was all that mattered; but in reality mother was a rather ragged speckled hen. She was, however, the most pugnacious, the most jealous and possessive hen on the farm, and that was why Charlie's father had shut her up inside a coop with a vast goose egg and kept her there until something happened. Each day she had been lifted off and the egg sprinkled with water to soften the shell. The summer had been dry that year, and all the early clutches of goose eggs had failed. This was very probably the last chance they had of rearing a goose for Christmas.

There had always been a goose for Christmas Day, Charlie's father said—a goose reared on their own corn and in their own orchard. So he had picked out the nastiest, broodiest hen in the yard to guard the egg and to rear his Christmas goose, and Charlie had sprinkled the egg each day.

When Charlie and his father first spied the golden gosling scavenging in the long grass with the speckled black hen clucking close by, they raced each other up the lane to break the good news to Charlie's mother. She pretended to be as happy about it all as they were, but in her heart of hearts she had been hoping that there would be no goose to rear and pluck that year. The job she detested most was fattening the goose for Christmas and then plucking it. The plucking took her hours, and the feathers flew everywhere, clouds of them—in her hair, down her neck. Her wrists and fingers ached with the work of it. But worst of all, she could not bear to look at the sweet, sad face she had come to know so well, hanging down over her knee, still smiling. She would willingly pluck a pheasant, a hen, even a woodcock; she would skin and gut a rabbit—anything but another goose.

Now Charlie's father was no fool and he knew his wife well enough to sense her disappointment. It was to soften the news, to console her and no doubt to persuade her again, that he suggested that Charlie might help this year. He had his arm round Charlie's shoulder, and that always made Charlie feel like a man.

'Charlie's almost ten now, lovely,' he said. Charlie's father always called his mother 'lovely,' and Charlie liked that. 'Ten years old next January, and he'll be as tall as you next Christmas. He'll be taller than me before he's through growing. Just look at him, he's grown an inch since breakfast.'

'I know Charlie's nearly ten, dear,' she said. 'I was there when he was born, remember?'

'Course you were, my lovely,' Charlie's father said, taking the drying-up cloth from her and sitting down at the kitchen table. 'I've got a plan, see. I known you've never been keen on rearing the goose for Christmas, and Charlie and me have been thinking about it, haven't we, Charlie?' Charlie hadn't a clue what his father was talking about, but he grinned and nodded anyway because it seemed the best thing to do. 'We thought that this year all three of us could look after the goose, you know, together like. Charlie boy can feed her up each day and drive her in each night. He can fatten her up for us. I'll kill her when the time comes—I know it seems a terrible thing to do, but what's got to be done has got to be done—and perhaps you wouldn't mind doing the little bit of plucking at the end for us. How would that be, my lovely?'

Charlie was flattered by the confidence his father had placed in him and his mother was, as usual, beguiled by both his Welsh tongue and the warmth of his smile. And so it was that Charlie came to rear the Christmas goose.

The fluffy, flippered gosling was soon exploring every part of the orchard and soon outgrew her bad-tempered foster mother. The hen shadowed her for as long as she could. Then she gave up and went back to the farmyard. The gosling turned into a goose, long and lovely and white. Charlie watched her grow. He would feed her twice a day, before and after school, with a little mixed corn. On fine autumn days he would sit with her in the orchard for hours at a time and watch her grazing under the trees. And he loved to watch her preening herself, her eyes closed in ecstasy as she curved her long neck and delved into the white feathers on her chest.

Charlie called the goose 'Gertrude' because she reminded him of his tall, lean Auntie Gertrude who always wore feathers in her hat in church. His aunt's nose was so imperial in shape and size that her neck seemed permanently stretched with the effort of seeing over it. But she was, for all that, immensely elegant and poised, so there could be no other name for the goose but Gertrude. And Gertrude moved through her orchard kingdom with an air of haughty indifference and an easy elegance that sets a goose apart from all other fowl. To Charlie, however, Gertrude had more than this. She had the gentle charm and sweetness of nature that Charlie warmed to as the autumn months passed.

They harvested cider apples in late October, so Gertrude's peace was disturbed each day for over two weeks as they climbed the lichen-coated apple trees and shook until the apples rained down on the grass. Gertrude and Charlie stood side by side waiting for the storm to pass, and then Charlie moved in to gather up the apples and fill the sacks. Gertrude stood back like a foreman and cackled encouragement from a distance. Her wings were fully grown now, and in her excitement she would raise herself to her full height, open her great white wings, stretch her neck, and beat the air with wild enthusiasm.

'It's clapping, she is,' said Charlie's father from high up in the tree. 'A grand bird. She's growing well. Be fine by Christmas if you look after her. We've got plenty of Bramley apples

this year, good for stuffing. Nothing like apple stuffing in a Christmas goose, is there, Charlie?'

The words fell like stones on Charlie's heart. As a farmer's son he knew that most of the animals on the farm went for slaughter. It was an accepted fact of life; neither a cause for sorrow nor rejoicing. Sick lambs, rescued piglets, ill suckling calves—Charlie helped to care for all of them and had already developed that degree of detachment that a farmer needs unless he is to be on the phone to the vet five times a day. But none of these animals were killed on the farm—they went away to be killed, and so he did not have to think about it. Charlie had seen his father shoot rats and pigeons and squirrels; but that again was different, they were pests.

Now, for the first time, as he watched Gertrude patrolling behind the dung heap, he realized that she had only two months to live, that she would be killed, hung up, plucked, pulled, stuffed and cooked, and borne in triumph onto the table on Christmas Day. 'Nothing like apple stuffing in a Christmas goose,'—his father's words would not go away.

Gertrude lowered her head and hissed at an intruding gaggle of hens that flew up in a panic and scattered into the hedgerow. She raised her wings again and beat them in a dazzling display before resuming her dignified patrol. She was magnificent, Charlie thought, a queen among geese. At that moment he decided that Gertrude was not going to be killed for Christmas. He would simply not allow it to happen.

With frosts and winds of November the last of the leaves were blown from the trees and swirled round the farmyard. Then the winter rains came and piled them into soggy mushy heaps against the hedgerows, clogging the ditches and filling the pot-holes. It was fine weather for a goose, though, and Gertrude revelled in the wildness of the winter winds. She stalked serenely through the leaves, her head held high against the wind and the rain, her feathers blown and ruffled.

Each day when Charlie got back from school he drove Gertrude in from the orchard to the safety of an empty calf pen. Foxes do come out on windy nights, and he did not want Gertrude taken by the fox any more than he wanted her carved up at Christmas. Before breakfast every morning Charlie opened the calf pen, and the two of them walked side by side out into the orchard where he emptied the scoop of corn into Gertrude's bowl. He talked to her all the while of the great master-plan he had dreamed up and how she must learn not to cackle too loudly. 'Won't be long now, Gerty,' he said. 'But if you make too much noise, you're done for. Your goose will be cooked, and that's for sure.' But Gerty wasn't listening. She had found a leafy puddle and was busy drinking from it, dipping and lifting her head, dipping and lifting . . .

Until late November his father had not taken much interest in Gertrude's progress, but now with Christmas only six weeks away he was asking almost daily whether or not Gertrude would be fat enough in time. 'She'll do better on oats, Charlie,' he said one breakfast. 'And I think you ought to shut her up now, and I don't mean just at night. I mean all the time. This wandering about in the orchard is all very well, but she won't put on much weight that way. There won't be much left on her for us, will there? You leave her in the calf pen from now on and feed her up.'

'She wouldn't like that,' Charlie said. 'You know she wouldn't. She likes her freedom. She'd pine away inside and lose weight.' Charlie had his reasons for wanting to keep Gertrude out in the orchard by day.

'Charlie's right, dear,' his mother said softly. 'Of course you're both right, really.' His mother was the perfect diplomat. 'Gertrude will fatten up better inside, but its lean meat we want, not fat. The more natural food she eats and the happier she is, the better she'll taste. My father used to say, "A happy goose is a tender goose." And anyway, there's only the three of us on Christmas Day, and Aunt Gertrude, of course. What would we do with a fifteen-pound goose?'

'All right, my lovely,' said Charlie's father. 'I know better than to argue when you and Charlie get together. But feed her on oats, Charlie, else there'll be nothing on her but skin and bone. And remember I have to kill her about a week

before Christmas—a goose needs a few days to hang. And then you'll need a day or so for plucking and dressing, won't you, lovely? I can smell it already,' he said, closing his eyes and sniffing the air. 'Goose and apple stuffing, roast potatoes, sprouts and chipolata sausages. Oh Christmas is coming and the goose is getting fat!'

The days rolled by into December, and Christmas beckoned. There was a Nativity play at school in which Charlie played Joseph. There was the endless shopping expeditions into town when Charlie dragged along behind his mother, who would never make up her mind about anything. Christmas with all its heady excitement meant little to Charlie that year for all he could think of was Gertrude. Again and again he went over the rescue plan in his mind until he was sure he had left nothing to chance.

December 16th was the day Charlie decided upon. It was a Saturday, so he would be home all day. But more important, that morning, Charlie knew his father would be out following the hunt five miles away at Dolton. He had asked Charlie if he wanted to go with him, but Charlie said he had to clean out Gertrude's pen. 'It's a pity you can't come,' said his father. 'Lovely frosty morning. There'll be a fine scent.'

Charlie watched from the farm gate until his father rattled off down the lane in the battered Land Rover. Then Charlie wasted no time. It was a long walk down to the river and he had to make a detour through the woods out of sight in case his mother spotted him.

Gertrude was waiting by the door of the calf pen as usual, impatient to get out into the orchard. But this morning she was not allowed to stop by her bowl of corn. Instead she was driven firmly out into the field beyond the orchard. She protested noisily, cackling and hissing, trying to get back by turning this way and that. But Charlie paid no attention. He banged his stick on the ground to keep her moving on. 'It's for your own good, Gerty, you'll see,' he said. 'It has to be far away to be safe. It's a hiding place no one will ever find. No one goes there in the winter, Gerty. You'll be as safe as houses down there, and no one will eat you for Christmas. Next year you'll be too tough to eat anyway. They say a goose can live for forty years. Think of that—not six months but forty years. So stop making a fuss, and walk on.'

He talked to her all the way down through Watercress Field, into Little Wood and out into Lower Down. By the time they reached the Marsh, Gertrude was exhausted and had stopped her cackling. Every gateway was a trial, with the puddles iced over. Try as she did, the goose could not keep her balance. She slithered and slipped across the ice until she found the ground rough and hard under her feet again. All the while the stick beat the ground behind her so that she could not turn around and go home. The fishing hut stood only a few yards from the river, an ugly building, squat and corrugated, but ideal for housing a refugee goose.

In the last few days Charlie had moved out all the fishing tackle. He had laid a thick carpet of straw on the floor so that Gertrude would be warm and comfortable. In one corner was the old hip bath he had found in the attic. The bath was brim full of water and Charlie had hitched a ramp over the side. By the door was a feeding trough already full of corn. But Gertrude was not impressed by her new home. She walked straight to the darkest end of the hut and hissed angrily at Charlie. He rattled the trough to show her where the corn was, but the goose looked away disdainfully. Her whole routine had been rudely disturbed and all she wanted to do was to sulk.

'You'll be all right, Gerty' said Charlie. 'But if you do hear anyone, don't start cackling. You've got food and water, and I'll be down to see you when I can. I can't come too often. It's a long way and they might get suspicious.' Gertrude hissed at him once again and turned her head away. 'I love you too!' said Charlie, and he went out bolting the door firmly behind him.

Charlie ran back all the way home because he needed to be breathless when he got there. His mother was just finishing icing the cake when Charlie came bursting in through the kitchen door. 'She's gone. Gertrude's gone. She's not in the orchard. She's not anywhere.'

Charlie and his mother searched all that morning and through the afternoon until the frost came down with the darkness and forced them to stop. Of course they found no sign of Gertrude.

'I can't understand it,' said Charlie's mother, as they broke the news to his father. 'She's just vanished. There's no feathers and no blood.'

'Well I can't believe it's a fox, anyway,' said Charlie's father. 'Not in broad daylight with a hunt just on the other side of the parish. She's in a hedge somewhere, laying an egg perhaps. They do that in winter sometimes, you know. She'll be back as soon as she gets hungry. It's a pity, though. She'll loose weight out in the cold.'

Charlie's mother was upset. 'We'll never find her if it snows. They've forecast snow tonight.'

And that night the snow did come. Snow upon snow. When Charlie looked out of his bedroom window the next morning, the farm had been transformed. Every muddy lane and rusty roof was immaculate with snow. Charlie was out early, as usual, helping his father feed the bullocks before breakfast. Then, saying he wanted to look for Gertrude, he set off towards the river, carrying a bucket of corn.

Gertrude hissed as he opened the door of the fishing hut, but when she saw who it was, she broke into an excited cackle and opened her wings in pure delight. She loved Charlie again. Charlie poured out the corn and topped up the water in the hip bath. 'So far, so good, Gerty,' he said. 'Not so bad in here, is it? Better in here than out. There's snow outside, but you'll be warm enough in here. Father thinks you're laying an egg in a hedge somewhere. Mother's worried sick about you. I can't tell her until after Christmas, though, 'cos she'd have to tell father. But she'll understand, and she'll make father understand, too. See you tomorrow, Gerty.'

Every day for a week, Charlie trudged down through the snow to feed Gertrude. By this time both his mother and father had given up all hope of ever finding their Christmas goose. 'It must have been a fox,' his mother reflected sadly. 'Gerty wouldn't just have walked off. But you'd think there would have been a tell-tale feather or two, wouldn't you? Don't be upset, Charlie.'

Charlie had always found it easy to bring tears to his eyes and he did so now. 'But she was my goose,' he sniffed. 'It was all my fault. I should have shut her up like father said.'

'Come on, Charlie', said his father, putting an arm round him. 'We can't have all these tears over a goose, now can we? After all we were going to eat her, and have you ever heard of anyone crying over Christmas dinner?'

Charlie was proud of his tearful performance, but was careful not to overdo it. 'I'll be all right,' he said manfully. 'I'm going to keep looking, though, just in case.'

One night, two days before Christmas, the wind changed from the north-east and rain came in from the west. By the morning, the snows had gone and the farm looked real and untidy again. Charlie could see the brook from his window.

But instead of a gentle burbling stream, the brook had turned into a raging brown torrent rushing down towards the river. The river! If the river burst its bank the fishing hut would be under water, Gertrude would be trapped inside. She wasn't used to swimming. Her feathers would be waterlogged and she would drown.

He dressed quickly and within minutes was running down towards the river. As he opened the gate into the marsh, he could see that the hut was completely surrounded by water and that the door was wide open. He splashed through the floods, praying that he would find Gertrude still alive and safe. But Gertrude wasn't even there. The trough and the straw floated in a foot of muddy water, but of Gertrude there was neither sound nor sight.

Somehow the door had opened and Gerty had escaped. He must have forgotten to bolt it, and the force of the flood water had done the rest. Now Gertrude was out there somewhere in the floods on her own. This time she had really escaped and when Charlie cried he really meant it, and the tears flowed uncontrollably.

Charlie spent the rest of the day searching the banks of the river for Gertrude, calling everywhere for her. But it was no use. The river was still high and flowing fast. He could only think that she had been swept away in the floods and drowned. He was filled with a sense of hopeless despair and wretchedness. He longed to tell his mother, but of course he could not. He dared not even show his feelings.

In the evening Aunty Gertrude arrived, for it

was Christmas Eve. A tree was brought in and together they decorated it before joining the carol singers in the village. But Charlie's heart was not in any of it. He went to bed and fell asleep without even putting his stocking out.

But when he awoke on Christmas morning the first thing he noticed was his stocking standing stiff as a sentry by his bedside table. Intrigued and suddenly excited, he felt to see what was inside the stocking. All he found was a tangerine and a piece of long, stiff card. He pulled out the card and looked at it. On it was written:

To Charlie, from Father Christmas:
> Goosey Goosey Gander, where shall I
> wander?
> From the orchard to the fishing hut,
> From the fishing hut to the hay-barn . . .

It was clearly his mother's handwriting.

Charlie tiptoed downstairs in his dressing gown, slipped on his wellingtons and then ran out across the back yard to the hay-barn. He unlatched the little wooden door and stepped inside. In the farthest corner, penned up against a wall of hay were two tall geese that cackled and hissed at his approach. They sidled away together into the hay, their heads almost touching. Charlie crept closer. One was a splendid grey goose he had never seen before. But the other looked distinctly familiar. And when she stretched out her white wings, there could be no doubt that this was Gertrude.

But his attention was drawn to a beautifully decorated card which read:

To Dearest Charlie from Gertrude,
I've got a message from your mother and father. Your mother says you should remember that if you walk in snow you leave footprints that can be followed. And your father says: Nice try, Charlie boy. We're having chicken for lunch today. Aunty Gertrude likes it better, anyway. Look after the geese. You'd better. They're yours for keeps!
So Charlie, meet Berty—he's a gander. He's my husband, Charlie, a present from

Father Christmas, and I hope you like him as much as I do. Oh, and by the way, thanks for saving my neck. I couldn't have asked for a better friend.
Much love for Christmas,
Gerty

By the time Charlie got back to the house, everyone was sitting down in the kitchen and having breakfast. Aunty Gertrude wished him a Happy Christmas and asked him what he'd had in his stocking. 'A goose, Aunty,' he said, smiling. 'And a tangerine!'

Charlie looked at his mother and then at his father. Both were trying hard not to laugh. 'Happy Christmas, Charlie boy, any sign of Gertrude yet?' his father asked.

'Yes,' said Charlie, swallowing his excitement. 'Father Christmas found her and brought her back—and Berty too—her husband, you know. Nice of him, wasn't it?'

'Gertrude?' said Aunt Gertrude, looking bewildered. 'A goose in your stocking?' She looked over her nose just like a certain goose. 'I don't understand. What's this all about?'

'Later, dear,' said Charlie's mother, gently patting her sister's arm. 'I'll tell you about it later, after we've eaten our Christmas dinner!'

The Mystery of Eilean Mor

Seventeen miles west of the Isle of Lewis, the largest Island of the Outer Hebrides, lie the seven Flannan Isles. They are little more than large rocks jutting out of the sea, but they are a menace to shipping.

For this reason it was decided to build a lighthouse on the largest of the islands—Eilean Mor. The work began in 1895. First a landing place was blasted out of solid rock, and steps were cut in the side of the cliff. These led to a steep path that wound up to the high, flat top of the island.

A winch for hauling up stores and supplies was mounted about twenty metres above the landing place. In a niche in the rocks, there was a heavy wooden box which contained the ropes and winding gear for the winch.

It took more than four years to build the lighthouse on such a remote and wind-swept place, but at last in 1899 the work was completed. The lighthouse tower, some twenty metres high, stood sixty-five metres above sea level. The light itself had an oil-burning lamp of 140,000 candle power, and was visible for forty miles.

In the year 1900, a passing ship reported that the light was out on the night of 15–16 December. The relief ship *Hesperus* was due to sail across to Eilean Mor with a keeper to replace one of the men in the lighthouse for the Christmas period. Because of bad weather, the ship was prevented from setting out for several days.

It was not until 26 December that the *Hesperus* hove-to off the landing stage. Aboard the ship the relief keeper, Joseph Moore, stared up anxiously at the lighthouse and the steep, rugged pathway leading up to it.

Why had no one from the island acknowledged the greeting signals hoisted by the *Hesperus*? Why was there no one waiting on the landing stage to help him when he was rowed across from the ship?

Jumping ashore without the aid of a line, Joseph Moore made his way up the path to the lighthouse. He tried to dismiss uneasy thoughts from his mind. Surely nothing was wrong? After all, it *was* Boxing Day. Surely his three friends would be there to greet him?

He was wrong. The lighthouse was deserted. The three keepers, Ducat, Marshall, and McArthur, had disappeared. Moore hurriedly called men from the *Hesperus*. Together they searched the island, but they could find no trace of the missing men.

The bewildered searchers returned to the lighthouse. Nothing inside gave any clue. The last entry in the log-book had been made for 9 am on Saturday 15 December. The lamps had been trimmed and cleaned, the oil reservoirs were filled, and the lens polished. The pots and pans in the kitchen had been washed, and everything had been neatly put away.

Then it was noticed that Ducat's and Marshall's sea-boots and oilskins were missing, yet McArthur's were found in their usual place. Even more strange was the discovery that the heavy wooden box containing the ropes and winch-gear was also missing.

It was noticed, too, that part of the railings leading down the zig-zag steps to the landing stage had been damaged, and a large block of stone had been dislodged from the cliff.

Did this mean that the three men had simply been washed off the landing stage by a violent wave?

At first it was thought that this was the explanation for the strange affair. But then people began to have second thoughts.

After all, if the three men *had* gone down to the landing stage in bad weather, they would surely all have worn their oilskins. Why were McArthur's still hanging in their usual place?

There had indeed been a number of storms that month and there had been very bad weather on the 12–13 of December. However, by the fifteenth, the storms had died away and the seas had been fairly calm. Surely then, three experienced men had not gone down to the landing stage together and all been washed away?

Another puzzling question is what happened to the heavy box of winching equipment? Had it been carried down the steps to the landing stage for some reason, and if so, why?

Many theories have been put forward to try and explain what happened. None of them solves the mystery completely.

Could one of the keepers have gone mad, murdered the others, and then thrown the bodies and himself into the sea? The tidy appearance of the lighthouse, and the neat, regular entries of the log-book make this theory unlikely.

Could one keeper have gone to the landing place and been washed off by a freak wave? Could the others have lost their lives trying to save him? Could this be possible, even though the landing stage could not be seen from the lighthouse?

Could all three keepers have noticed something unusual in the sea and all three gone to investigate? In fact it has been observed that, even on calm days, a freak of the tide causes the sea level to rise suddenly without warning and, almost at once, to fall gently away again. Could such a freak surge of water have plucked the men into the sea?

But why then was McArthur not in his oilskins and why was the heavy box missing? Why had the men not simply taken the rope that was inside it?

If the sea did not claim the lives of the three men, did they die by other means? If so, what are they?

Whatever the true facts are, they will remain for ever shrouded in mystery.

Who was King Wenceslas?

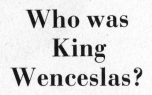

We sing about Good King Wenceslas in one of our best loved Christmas carols. But who *was* the monarch who 'looked out on the Feast of Stephen'?

WE GO BACK TO 924 A.D. THE COUNTRY OF BOHEMIA IN CENTRAL EUROPE IS TORN WITH STRIFE AND UNREST...

KING VRATISLAV OF BOHEMIA HAS BEEN MURDERED AND HIS YOUNG SON, WENCESLAS, IS TO SUCCEED HIM.

BUT THE YOUNG BOY'S LIFE IS IN DANGER. HIS GRANDMOTHER, LUDMILA, TRIES TO PROTECT HIM.

BUT GRANDMOTHER, IF I AM KING, SURELY I MUST STAY HERE IN PRAGUE?

NO, WENCESLAS, YOU ARE TOO YOUNG AND HAVE MANY ENEMIES! THERE IS DANGER ON ALL SIDES...

WENCESLAS'S OWN MOTHER, DRAHOMIR, HATES HIM. SHE WANTS HER OTHER SON, BOLESLAS, TO BE KING.

WE MUST RID OURSELVES OF WENCESLAS. BOLESLAS MUST BECOME KING IN HIS PLACE!

LUDMILA IS TOO STRONG. BUT ONE DAY...

143

Boxing Day

Boxing Day takes its name from the ancient practice of opening boxes which contained money given to those who had given their service during the year. It was also the day when alms boxes, placed in churches on Christmas Day, were opened. The money was then given to the priest or used to help the poor and needy. Another name for Boxing Day used to be Offering Day.

The earliest boxes of all were not box shaped, as you might imagine, nor were they made of wood. They were, in fact, earthenware containers with a slit in the top (rather like piggy banks). These earthenware 'boxes' were used by the Romans for collecting money to help pay for the festivities at the winter Saturnalia celebrations.

It is possible that this type of money-box was introduced into Britain by the Romans. Such 'boxes' may have been used by the early church leaders to collect alms money.

But it is certain that during the seventeenth century it became the custom for apprentices to ask their master's customers for money at Christmas time. They collected this money in earthenware containers, which could be opened only by being smashed, and on Boxing Day the apprentices would eagerly have a 'smashing time' seeing how much they had collected.

Gradually the practice of receiving a gift of money at Christmas grew to include all those who had given good service throughout the year.

Boxing Day is really St Stephen's Day. St Stephen is the patron saint of horses, and 26 December has always had a close connection with horses. It is traditional for horses and hounds to meet on village greens and in some parts of Europe there are horse festivals and race meetings. In other places farmers still decorate their horses and take them to church to be blessed.

At one time it was a widespread practice to let blood out of horses on St Stephen's Day. It was thought that 'bleeding' an animal improved its health and strength.

No one knows if St Stephen's Day belongs to the first Christian Martyr who was stoned to death about AD 33, or to another Stephen who first took the gospel to Sweden and was killed there in the eleventh century.

According to legend, St Stephen of Sweden loved horses. He had five of his own: two chestnut, two white and one dappled. By riding each in turn, Stephen was able to travel great distances on his missionary journeys. One day, while riding through a lonely forest, he was murdered by a band of men who tied his body on to the back of a wild, unbroken colt. 'That horse will gallop until it drops,' cried the men, 'and no one will ever find the bodies!'

However the horse did not bolt into the wilderness, but carried Stephen gently back to his home at Norrtälje. Stephen's grave became a shrine to which sick horses and other animals were taken for healing.

Candles

Candles have always played an important part in the observance of Christmas. To many people the candle symbolizes Christ: the wax represents His body; the wick, His soul; and the flame, His divine nature.

In the middle ages it was the custom to light an enormous candle called the Christmas candle which burned each evening to cast its glow on the Yuletide festivities.

In many countries, candles are burned in the window to guide strangers. In Ireland, candles are lit on Christmas Eve and left shining all night in a window. The door is left open symbolically to welcome the Holy Family in case they are seeking shelter.

The Christmas candles placed on Advent wreaths, Christmas trees, and kissing bushes are usually red. White candles, symbolizing the purity of the Virgin Mary, are always used in churches and religious ceremonies.

The Scandinavian countries have many delightful traditions in which candles are used.

In Sweden, Christmas begins with the Saint Lucia ceremony. Before dawn on the morning of 13 December, the youngest daughter from each family puts on a long white robe with a red sash. On her head she wears a crown of evergreens with tall lighted candles attached to it. She wakes her parents, and serves them with coffee and Lucia buns. The other children in the family accompany her, and the boys dress as 'star boys' in long white shirts and pointed hats.

Saint Lucia processions are held all over Sweden at schools, offices, and shopping centres. The custom goes back to Lucia, a Christian virgin martyred for her beliefs at Syracuse in the fourth century. The Saint Lucia ceremony is fairly recent, but it represents the traditional thanksgiving for the return of the sun.

Candle-lit processions to Church feature in Scandinavian Christmases, where, in the home, it is the mother who always lights the candles on Christmas Eve.

Make your own Christmas Candles

You will need:
disposable plastic moulds from
  mousses, frozen juice cartons,
  or cottage cheese cartons
paraffin wax (which you can
  usually buy from the chemist)
  or old candle ends
wax crayons
an old saucepan
empty tins which are clean
a large tin tray
a little cooking oil
a few heavy buttons
heat-proof gloves
a bowl of cold water
several strips of cardboard.

Grease the moulds with cooking
oil. Put the tins on the tray. Place
one crayon of each colour into a
tin. Melt the candles and wax
crayons in the saucepan.
Carefully remove the old wicks.

If they are long enough, you can
use the wicks for your new
candles; otherwise make string
wicks. Tie one end of the wick
onto a button and place the
button in the bottom of the
mould. Place the mould in a
bowl of cold water. When all the
moulds are prepared, put on the
gloves. Pour hot wax from the
saucepan onto the crayons in the
tins. Stir to mix the colour into
the wax. Then pour it into the
moulds.

Make a cardboard bridge to go
across the mould. About half-
way along the bridge make a
short slit that will hold the wick
straight. Slip the wick in place
and fix the bridge onto the sides
of the mould. Leave in the cold
water to set. After two hours, top
up the well which forms in the
centre with wax that is left over.
Leave overnight. Remove the
candle from the mould by
dipping it into hot water to
loosen the wax.

If you want specially decorated
candles, use warm wax to stick
on ornaments, cut-out pictures,
pieces of gold doiley, ribbons, or
sequins, held in place with map-
pins or half-inch sequin pins.
You can scratch out patterns with
a knitting needle, and rub paint
into them.

If you have a flower press why
not use some of your flowers to
decorate the sides of candles.
You will need to put them on
with a brush dipped in hot wax,
so it is wise for small children to
have an adult with them. Brush a
small amount of hot clear wax
where the flower is to go, and
press it on quickly. To set the
flower into place, lightly brush
another layer of wax over it. The
wax should be quite hot, as cool
wax causes a thick cloudy film to
cover the flower.

If you want a snow candle, heat
clear wax. When it has melted,
allow it to cool slightly and whip
it with an egg-beater. Using a
fork, press the whipped wax. For
a snowball candle, use an old
ball for a mould. Cut it in half
and fill each half with wax.
When it has set, cut a shallow
groove down the middle of one

side and put in the wick. Brush
both sides with warm wax and
put them together. Press warm
whipped wax all over the outside
of the snowball.

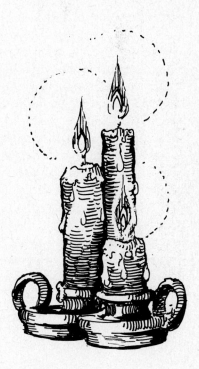

Epiphany and Twelfth Night

The story of the coming of the Wise Men to pay homage to the Holy Child creates one of the most beautiful and significant of all the images in the Christmas story.

Three strangers arrive mysteriously at the stable in Bethlehem. They have travelled for many days from far-off lands. Their course has been set by the position of a star which they observed rising in the East.

The strangers' rich and splendid clothes contrast strongly with those of the shepherds who kneel nearby. They bow low before Mary and the Child, and on the ground they lay gifts of gold, frankincense, and myrrh.

Who were these mysterious strangers? Where had they come from? In the Bible it is only in Saint Matthew's Gospel that we read about them. He refers to them as astrologers or wise men, and not as kings as they are so often portrayed.

In fact, no one really knows the whole story, nor even how many Wise Men there were. In Matthew's story there is no mention of their number, although it is assumed that there were three because of the three gifts that they brought.

By the sixth century, however, they were thought of as being three kings. As time passed, various legends grew up around them. They came to be identified as Melchior, ruler of Nubia and Arabia; Balthazar, ruler of Ethiopia; and Caspar, ruler of Tarsus.

Traditionally they symbolize three stages of life: Melchior is a wise old man with a long beard. Balthazar is a dark-skinned man of about forty. And Caspar is a tall, beardless youth of about twenty.

Their gifts are also symbolic: gold was given as a tribute to Christ as the King; frankincense in recognition of His Divine Nature; and myrrh as a sign of His death.

The Wise Men are often referred to as Magi, which is a name given to an order of ancient Medes and Persians. All Magi were men of great learning, and they were skilled astrologers and astronomers.

There is evidence to believe that there *was* a very bright star seen about the time of the birth of Jesus. It is also possible that the Wise Men knew of the Jewish prophecy that a new star would appear to herald the coming of salvation for the world.

For years the Magi had patiently watched the sky and when at last the star appeared, they set out to find the King who was to redeem mankind.

When they arived at Jerusalem, the Wise Men went to Herod to ask him where the King of the Jews had been born. Inwardly Herod seethed with rage and jealousy, but at once he ordered a search to be made of the scriptures. A reference to Bethlehem was found, and Herod sent the Wise Men there, hoping by this means to identify the Baby and kill Him.

The Bible says that the Wise Men were warned in a dream not to return to Herod, and departed from the country by another route.

6 January is the Feast of the Epiphany, which commemorates the visit of the Wise Men to the Infant Jesus. It is one of the earliest of all Christian celebrations.

In some countries, Epiphany is an important part of the Christmas festival. In Spain, on Epiphany Eve, the children put their shoes on the balcony or windowsill. During the night the three Wise Men will pass by on their way to Bethlehem. They will carry gifts with them. The children leave hay in the shoes for the hungry camels. In the morning the hay is gone, and the children's shoes are overflowing with presents.

Italian children look forward to the coming of a kindly old witch called La Befana, who rides on a broomstick and brings them presents.

The name Befana comes from Epiphania (Epiphany). According to a legend, La Befana was too busy doing her housework to offer the Wise Men hospitality when they called at her house. 'I'm too busy now,' she grumbled, 'I'll see them when they come back!' But the Wise Men went home by a different route, and she never saw them again. As a punishment, she searches for ever for the Baby Jesus and leaves a present in every house, in case he is there.

Epiphany Eve coincides with Twelfth Night which marks the end of Christmas. Twelfth Night used to be a time of great celebration in Britain, probably because at one time people considered it to be Christmas Eve. After the Gregorian calendar was introduced in 1752,

twelve days were 'lost'. But for many years people refused to recognize the new dates and insisted on celebrating Christmas on Twelfth Day.

In the country, Twelfth Night was the time to ask for a plentiful and fruitful year. In some parts it was the custom to go into the orchards and 'wassail' the fruit trees. This involved drinking the health of every tree. Then everyone would throw part of the drink, followed by stones or even gunshot, through the bare branches of each tree. It was thought that this would drive away any evil spirits which might be lurking in the orchard. Sometimes the farmer and his family would solemnly bow to the trees. If corn was grown as well, spiced ale would be sprinkled over the ground.

> Apples and pears and right good corn,
> Come in plenty to every one,
> Eat and drink good cake and hot ale,
> Give Earth to drink and she'll not fail.

If the farmer kept animals, a health was drunk to each one to make sure of a safe and healthy year.

Another interesting custom used to be 'Finding the King of the Beans'. A special 'Twelfth Night' cake was baked which contained a single bean. The finder of the bean became King or Queen for the evening and was expected to preside over the merrymaking.

149

Christmas Presents

Have you ever noticed how grown-ups give each other presents?
There's no mystery in it, and not a lot of fun.

Every year Grandma gets a tin of talcum
   powder.
She always says, 'Ah my favourite!'
Even before she opens the wrapping.
Grandpa always says, 'Well, I know what's in here.
   'It's two pairs of socks. Just what I wanted!'

This year, Aunti Vi had an umbrella
   in an umbrella-shaped parcel.
I mean, it *looked* just like an umbrella.
And, before Aunti Vi pulled the paper off,
   she said to Mum, 'It will match that new coat
   of mine.'

As for Mum and Dad, they just sat there and
   said,
'We've given each other a joint present this year.
   It's a digital clock-radio for our bedroom.'
Do you know, they didn't even bother to wrap it
   up and put it under the tree!

At the end, when everything had been given out,
Mum said, 'We mustn't forget the gift-vouchers
   from Debbie and Jim. We sent them a cheque
   for the same amount. We always do.'
I call that a bit unimaginative, don't you?

Maybe, when you come to think about it,
Grown-ups need Father Christmas far more
   than children do.

Seeing in the New Year

There is a good reason why the Romans named the first month of the year after the god Janus. In Roman mythology Janus was the god who presided over all beginnings. Doors and gates were under his special care, which is why he has two faces: one at the front and one at the back of his head, so that he can look both ways at once. The Romans thought of him as opening the door of the year to let the old year out and the new year in.

For most people, the New Year is a time to make a fresh start or to begin again with fresh determination. They make resolutions to do better or to try harder. In earlier times, superstitious country folk thought that their lives were governed by nature, and they practised all kinds of customs to do with the very first things of the New Year. For example, the first bucket of water to be drawn from the well was thought to have special powers.

In Scotland, the New's Eve, or Hogmanay as it is called, is celebrated with more enthusiasm than Christmas. It is considered very important to let the new year in, and *'first footing'* is a custom that still flourishes. There is an old saying: 'The first foot over the threshold decides the luck of the year!'

So, just before the clock strikes twelve on New Year's Eve, the family waits in silence. At the last stroke of midnight, there is a loud knock at the door. This is opened to reveal a tall, dark stranger. He must be carrying a piece of mistletoe, a lump of coal, and some money. Then the stranger must enter without a word, put the coal on the fire, the money on the table, and the mistletoe on the mantelpiece. Then he wishes everyone a Happy New Year. The silence is broken, and everyone drinks a toast to the New Year and eats the special cakes made for the occasion.

There are many slight variations from place to place on the items the stranger must carry, but almost everywhere it is agreed that he must be dark-haired. But he must not be flat-footed, nor cross-eyed. If his eyebrows meet this is sure to be the sign of an unhappy year.

In Scotland gifts are exchanged on New Year's Day. This was once a general custom. In particular, lords and noblemen gave lavish presents to the sovereigns of the land. In the fourteenth century, rich husbands gave their wives costly hairpins. Sometimes money was given instead, and this was called 'pin money'.

The Mummers' Play

Mumming plays are one of the oldest surviving features of the traditional English Christmas. Mumming goes back for over a thousand years, and the plays are intended to show the struggle between good and evil.

The characters vary from play to play, although the hero is always St George, who fights with the power of evil traditionally represented by the Turkish Knight.

Another important character is the doctor, who is called upon to revive the wounded St George with his magic potions.

Two other figures appear in most mummers' plays. One is Father Christmas. The other is Johnny Jack. Johnny Jack's function was to appear at the end of the play to ask for money. His costume was usually hung with a number of rag dolls to represent his many children and to appeal to the rich for charity at Christmas time.

THE MUMMERS' CHORUS

sung before entering the house

God bless the Master of this house,
We hope he is within.
And if he is pray tell us so,
And soon we will begin.

With a hey dum dum, with a hey dum dum,
With a hey dum dum de derry:
For we come this Christmas time,
A-purpose to be merry.

We hope the Mistress is within,
A-sitting by the fire,
A-pitying we poor mummers here,
Out in the dirty mire. (*chorus*)

We don't come here but once a year,
And hope 'tis no offence.
But if it is pray tell us so,
And we will soon go hence. (*chorus*)

(*There is a loud knocking at the door.*
Father Christmas enters.)

FATHER CHRISTMAS:
Room, room, brave gallants . . . room! I am just come to show you some merry sport and game to help pass away this cold winter's day. Old activity, new activity, such activity as never been seen before, and perhaps will never be seen any more.
For here come I, Old Father Christmas.
Christmas is Christmas, welcome or welcome not.
I hope Old Father Christmas will never be forgot.
All in this room there will be shown,
The dreadfullest battle that ever was known.
So walk in, St George, with thy free heart,
And see if thou cans't claim peace
for thine own part.
   (*Enter St George*)

ST GEORGE:
In comes I, St George.
A man of courage bold.
With my broad sword and my spear,
I won ten crowns of gold.
Where is the man that now will me defy?
I'll cut him full of holes,
And make his buttons fly!
   (*Enter Turkish Knight*)

TURKISH KNIGHT:
In come I, the Turkish Knight.
Just come from Turkeyland to fight.
I will fight thee, St George,
Thou man of courage bold.
If thy blood be hot,
I will quickly fetch it cold.

ST GEORGE:
Hello, my little fellow.
Thou talkest very bold.
Just like the little Turkey
As I have once been told.
Therefore, Turkish Knight,
Draw forth thy sword and fight.
Pull out thy purse and pay.
I will have satisfaction
Before thou goest away!

TURKISH KNIGHT:
Satisfaction! No satisfaction at all!
My hand is made of iron,
My body lined with steel,
And I will battle thee to see
Which on the ground shall fall.
    (*They fight. The Turkish Knight falls.*)

ST GEORGE:
Oh, and behold!
And see what I have done,
The Turkey Knight falls to the ground,
Just like the evening sun.
I have a little bottle in my pocket
Called elecampaign.
One drop on the rough of this man's tongue,
Will raise him up to fight again.
    (*The Turkish Knight rises to his knees.*)

TURKISH KNIGHT:
Oh pardon me, St George.
Oh pardon me I crave.
Oh pardon me this once,
And I will be thy slave.

ST GEORGE:
No pardon shalt thou have,
While I have foot to stand.
So rise thee up again,
And fight on, sword in hand!

(*They fight again. The Turkish Knight is killed. Enter Turkish Knight's Father.*)

TURKISH KNIGHT'S FATHER:
St George, St George, what hast thou done?
Thou hast out and slain my only son.
Is there a doctor to be found
To cure this man lying bleeding on the ground?
    (*Enter Doctor*)

DOCTOR:
Oh yes, there is a doctor to be found
To cure this man a-bleeding on the ground.

TURKISH KNIGHT'S FATHER:
What is thy fee, Doctor?

DOCTOR:
Ten guineas is my fee.
Fifteen I will take of thee
Before I set this gallant free.

TURKISH KNIGHT'S FATHER:
Take it, Doctor, but what cans't thou cure?

DOCTOR:
The ague, the palsy, the gout,
The pain that is within and without.
If thou breakest thy neck or arm.
I will stoutly set it again.
Bring me an old woman of fourscore years
and ten,
Without a tooth in her head,
I will fetch her young and plump again.

TURKISH KNIGHT'S FATHER:
A clever doctor thou be
If this be true that thou sayest to me.

DOCTOR:
What I do, I do before thy very eyes,
And if thou cans't not believe it, 'tis a very
hard case.
I have a little bottle in my pocket
Called golden foster-drops . . .
One drop on this man's tongue,
Another on his crown,
Will strike a beat throughout the heart
And rise him off the ground.

ST GEORGE:
Arise thou cowardly dog! Go home to thine own country and tell them what old England has done for thee, and say that I will fight ten thousand better men than thee.
(*Turkish Knight and Father exeunt.*)

ST GEORGE:
Now on this spot, I, good St George,
That worthy champion stand.
For I have fought the Turkish Knight,
And sent him from the land.
Now if any foe dare enter that door,
I'll hack him as small as dust
And send him to the cook shop
To be made into mince-pie crust.
(*Enter the Giant*)

GIANT:
Here come I, the giant,
Bold Tabberner is my name.
In all the lands where I hold sway,
They tremble at my fame.
Where'er I go, they tremble at my sight.
No champion long with me can fight!

ST GEORGE:
Here's one that dares to look thee in the face,
And soon I'll send thee to another place.
(*They fight. The Giant is killed. St George is wounded.*)

FATHER CHRISTMAS:
Is there a Doctor to be found,
All ready, near at hand,
To cure a deep and deadly wound
And make the champion stand?

DOCTOR:
Here am I, the Doctor,
All ready, near at hand.
I will cure the deadly wound,
And make the champion stand!

FATHER CHRISTMAS:
What is thy fee?

DOCTOR:
Fifteen guineas is my fee!
Ten guineas to thee.

I have here a bottle of poulton's potion,
One draft will fetch him right again
I have a notion.
(*St George drinks the medicine.*)

ST GEORGE: (*getting up*)
On this spot, I, brave St George,
That worthy champion stand.
Neither Turkish Knight, nor Giant bold
Could stay against my hand.
Now should any foe dare come in
I'll knock his eyeballs from his head,
And pierce him through the skin!
(*Enter the King of Egypt*)

KING OF EGYPT:
Here I, the King of Egypt, do appear.
The dragon slay, St George,
And claim my daughter fair.

ST GEORGE:
I am the brave St George.
From Britain I did spring.
I'll fight the dragon bold,
The fight I'll soon begin.
I'll clip his wings. He shall not fly!
I'll cut him down, or else I'll die!
(*Enter the Dragon, followed by the King of Egypt's daughter with her hands bound together.*)

DRAGON:
Who's he that seeks the Dragon's blood
And dares to challenge me to fight?
That English dog!
I'll have him as a snack
Before I sup tonight!
(*They fight. The Dragon is killed, St George is wounded.*)

FATHER CHRISTMAS:
Is there a doctor to be found
All ready, near at hand,
To cure a deep and deadly wound
And make the champion stand?

DOCTOR:
Here am I, the Doctor,
All ready near at hand.
I will cure the deadly wound,
And make the champion stand!

FATHER CHRISTMAS:
What is thy fee?

DOCTOR:
Ten guineas my fee.
But this time it's free.
I have here a box of heapy's compound
A touch of this will raise him from the ground.

ST GEORGE: (*standing up*)
I've fought the fiery dragon
And brought him to the slaughter.

KING OF EGYPT: (*leading his daughter forward*)
By that you've won fair Sabra,
The King of Egypt's daughter.
 (*Enter Johnny Jack.*)

JOHNNY JACK:
In comes I, little Johnny Jack,
With my wife and family at my back.
My family large, tho' I am small,
So a very little helps us all.
Roast beef, plum-pudding and mince-pie,
Who like that any better than
Old Father Christmas and I.
A jug of Christmas ale, sir,
Will make us merry and sing.
Some money in our pocket
Is a very fine thing.
So, ladies and gentlemen, all at your ease,
Give the Christmas mummers just what you
please.

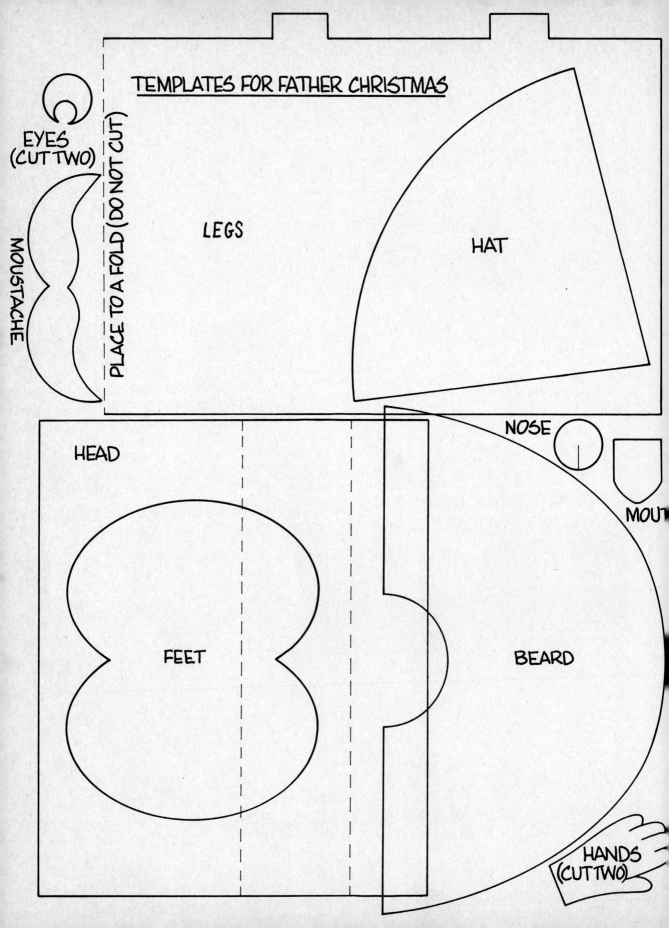

TEMPLATES FOR FATHER CHRISTMAS

EYES
(CUT TWO)

MOUSTACHE

PLACE TO A FOLD (DO NOT CUT)

LEGS

HAT

NOSE

MOUT

HEAD

FEET

BEARD

HANDS
(CUT TWO)

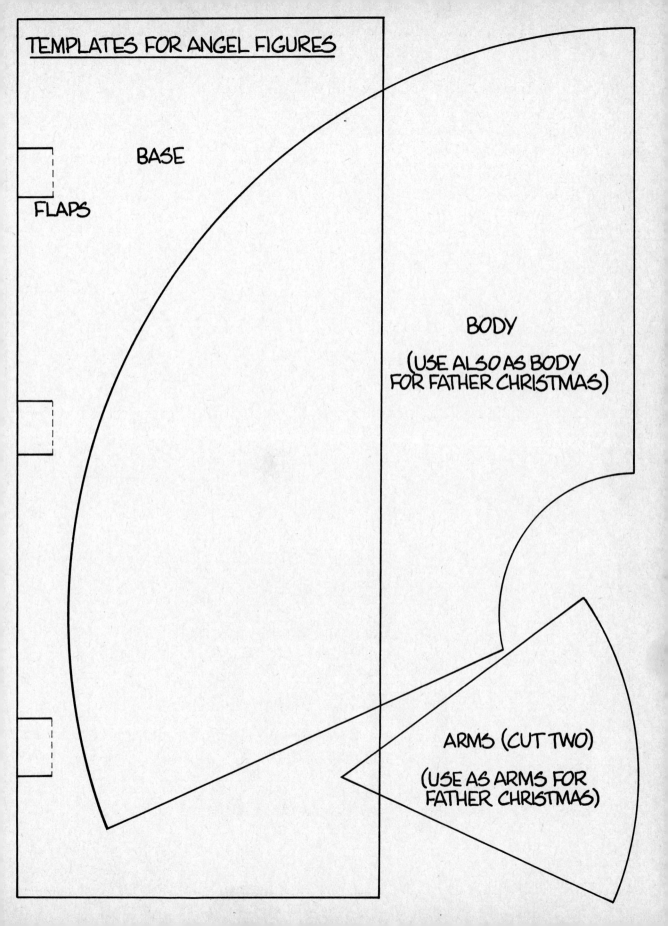

A five-pointed star is very difficult to draw, but it is a useful shape to use when you make Christmas cards, decorations or shapes for your biscuits. This template can be traced to give you six different sizes.

Solution to crossword on p. 129

¹M	²A	G	I		³G	⁴I	F	⁵T	S		⁶S	⁷T	⁸A	R
Y		A			O		A		T		⁹T	E	N	
¹⁰R	U	M		¹¹G	L	I	T	T	E	R		¹²A	T	E
R		E			D		H		P		¹³D		H	
¹⁴H	O	S	¹⁵T	S		¹⁶B	E	¹⁷T	H	L	E	H	E	¹⁸M
			A		¹⁹M	A	R	I	E		C		²⁰M	Y
²¹F	²²R	A	N	K	I	N	C	E	N	S	E			S
	E		N		N		H			M				T
	J		E		²³C	A	R	O	²⁴L		²⁵B	A	B	E
²⁶B	O	U	N	C	E		I		I		E			R
	I		B		P		S		²⁷N	²⁸O	R	²⁹W	³⁰A	Y
	³¹C	H	A	R	I	O	T	³²E	E	R		³³A	L	P
³⁴H	E		U		E		³⁵M	A	N	G	E	R		L
³⁶A	³⁷D	A	M			³⁸P	A	S		A				A
M		Y		³⁹G	L	A	S	T	O	N	B	U	R	Y

The Old Year Now Away is Fled

The Old Year now away is fled.
　　The New Year it is entered.
Then let us now our sins down tread,
　　And joyfully all appear.
Let's be merry on this holiday,
And let us now both sport and play.
Hang sorrow, let's cast care away,
　　God send you a Happy New Year.

(Tune: Greensleeves)

Acknowledgements

The editor and publishers gratefully acknowledge permission to reproduce the following copyright material:

Victor G Ambrus: *Dracula's Christmas* was specially drawn for this book. Copyright © 1981 Victor G Ambrus.   Sheila Cassidy: *Christmas in Prison* is taken from Cassidy: *Audacity to Believe* (Collins 1977). Copyright © 1977 Sheila Cassidy. Reprinted by permission of Anthony Sheil Associates Ltd.   Charles Causley: *At Nine of the Night*. From *Collected Poems* (Macmillan). Reprinted by permission of David Higham Associates Ltd.   Winifred Champ: *The Best Present of All* was specially written for this book. Copyright © 1981 Winifred Champ.   Christmas Crossword. Copyright © 1981 Jonathan Crowther.   Gillian Cross: *A Very Proper Christmas* was specially written for this book. Copyright © Gillian Cross.   Roy Fuller: *A Peculiar Christmas* and *The Real True Father Christmas* were specially written for this book. Copyright © 1981 Roy Fuller.   Colin Hawkins: *The Christmas Reindeer Flying School* was specially drawn for this book. Copyright © 1981 Colin Hawkins.   Penelope Hughes: *Christmas Time*, arranged by Sir David Willcocks. Copyright © 1981 Music Department, Oxford University Press. This simplified version is used by permission.   Eric James: *Christmas Presents* was specially written for this book. Copyright © 1981 Roderick Hunt.   C Day Lewis: *Christmas Tree*. From *Collected Poems 1954*. Reprinted by permission of the Executors of the Estate of C Day Lewis and the Hogarth Press and Jonathan Cape Ltd. as publishers.   Michael Morpurgo: *The Goose is Getting Fat* was specially written for this book. Copyright © Michael Morpurgo. By permission of A M Heath and Co Ltd.   John Press: *African Christmas*. Reprinted by permission of Oxford University Press.   Clive Sansom: *Winter Morning*. From *An English Year* (Chatto). Reprinted by permission of David Higham Associates Ltd.   Terry Tapp: *The Master's Gift* was specially written for this book. Copyright © 1981 Terry Tapp.   Bernard Taylor: *The Story of Prudence Trigg* is reprinted by permission of the author.   Anthony Thwaite: *Horace's Christmas Disappointment*. From *Allsorts 5* (Macmillan). Reprinted by permission of the author.   Keith Waterhouse: *Albert's Christmas Ship*. Reprinted by permission of the author.

We are grateful to The European School, Culham, for the Christmas letters.

The editor and publishers would like to thank Phyllis Porter for the Things to Make sections in this book.

While every effort has been made to secure permission, it has in a few cases proved impossible to trace the author or his executor. If any copyright holder not here acknowledged will contact the publishers, corrections will be made in future editions.

The publishers would like to thank the following for permission to reproduce photographs:

Australian Information Service, p.124; Barnaby's Picture Library, pp.125, 145; Bodleian Library, Oxford, p.121; Camera Press, p.91; Mary Evans Picture Library, pp.26, 27, 36, 42, 45, 79, 84, 110, 128; Finnish Tourist Board, p.82; The Fotomas Index, p.120; Grenfell Association of Great Britain and Ireland, p.37; Herts Advertiser, p.145; Illustrated London News, p.47; IPC Magazines, p.94; John Kerr, Felixstowe Times, p.15; Italian State Tourist Office (ENIT), p.116; Mansell Collection, pp.37, 44, 47, 48; Marcos Ortiz, pp.80, 81; Picturepoint, pp.33, 37, 45, 47, 106, 107; Royal Society for the Protection of Birds/M.W. Richards, p.113; Swedish Embassy/ Göran Algård, p.146; Tibbenham P.R. Ltd., p.43; John Topham, pp.82, 83; UNICEF, p.37; ZEFA/R. Holder, p.117.

Illustrations by Lynne Byrnes, Martin Cottam, Karen Daws, John Flynn, John Glover, Peter Gregory, Timothy Jacques, Susan Lacombe, Arthur Litchfield, Chris Molan, Trevor Parkin, Graham Round, Annabel Spenceley, Petula Stone, Martin White.

Additional photography by Dafydd Jones, Jericho Workshop.

Oxford University Press would like to wish all their contributors and readers a very Happy Christmas.